CROCHET DOILIES

To my daughter Alet

CROCHET DOILIES

Heila Klopper

Cape Town

Contents

Abbreviations

B – bobble(s)
beg – begin(ning)
ch – chain(s)
cl – cluster(s)
dc – double crochet
dec – decrease
dtr – double treble

foll – following
gp(s) – group(s)
htr – half treble(s)
inc – increase
p – picot(s)
rep – repeat
rnd(s) – round(s)

sh – shell(s)
sp – space(s)
ss – slip stitches(es)
st(s) – stitch(es)
tr – treble
unf – unfinished
yoh – yarn over hook

Doily with eight points

(see photograph on front cover)

MATERIALS: Approximately 30 g Pingouin no. 8; crochet hook 1,25 mm

SIZE: 27 cm in diameter

Commence with 8 ch, join with ss to form a ring.

1st rnd: 3 ch for 1st tr, 23 tr into ring, ss into 3rd ch.

2nd rnd: 3 ch into ss, 1 tr each into next 2 tr, * 3 ch, 1 tr into each of next 3 tr; rep from * all round, ss into 3rd ch.

3rd rnd: 3 ch into ss, * 2 tr into next tr, 1 tr into next tr, 4 ch, 1 tr into next tr; rep from *, ss into 3rd ch.

4th rnd: 3 ch into ss, 1 tr into next tr, * 2 ch, 1 tr each into next 2 tr, 2 ch, 1 tr into sp, 2 ch, 1 tr each into next 2 tr; rep from *, ss into 3rd ch.

5th rnd: 3 ch into ss, 1 tr into next tr, * 1 tr 2 ch and 1 tr into sp, 1 tr each into next 2 tr, 2 ch, 1 tr into next tr, 2 ch, 1 tr each into next 2 tr; rep from *, ss into 3rd ch.

6th rnd: 3 ch into ss, * 1 tr each into next 2 tr, 1 tr 3 ch and 1 tr into sp, 1 tr each into next 3 tr, 2 ch, 1 tr into next tr, 2 ch, 1 tr into next tr; rep from *, ss into 3rd ch.

7th to 12th rnd: As for 6th rnd, but inc as before at tr gps.

13th rnd: ss to tr, 3 ch into ss, 1 tr each into next 7 tr, * 2 ch, miss next tr, 1 tr 3 ch and 1 tr into 3 ch sp, 2 ch, miss next tr, 1 tr each into next 8 tr, 4 ch, miss next tr, 1 dc into next tr, 4 ch, miss next tr, 1 tr each into next 8 tr; rep from *, ss into 3rd ch.

14th rnd: ss to tr, 3 ch into ss, 1 tr each into next 5 tr, * 2 ch, miss next tr, 1 tr into sp, 2 ch, 1 tr 3 ch and 1 tr into next sp, 2 ch, 1 tr into next sp, 2 ch, miss next tr, 1 tr each into next 6 tr, 5 ch, miss next tr, 1 dc into 4 ch sp, 1 dc into dc, 1 dc into 4 ch sp, 5 ch, miss next tr, 1 tr each into next 6 tr; rep from *, ss into 3rd ch.

15th rnd: ss to tr, 3 ch into ss, 1 tr each into next 3 tr, * 2 ch, miss next tr, (1 tr into next sp, 2 ch) twice, 1 tr 3 ch and 1 tr into next sp, 2 ch 1 tr each into next 2 sps, 2 ch, miss next tr, 1 tr each into next 4 tr, 5 ch, miss next tr, 1 dc into next sp, 3 dc into next 3 dc, 1 dc into sp, 5 ch, miss next tr, 1 tr each into next 4 tr; rep from *, ss into 3rd ch.

16th rnd: ss to next tr, 3 ch into ss, 1 tr into next tr, * 2 ch, miss next tr, (1 tr into next sp, 2 ch) 3 times, 1 tr 3 ch and 1 tr into next sp (2 ch, 1 tr into next sp) 3 times, 2 ch, miss next tr, 1 tr each into next 2 tr, 6 ch, miss next tr, 1 dc into sp, 5 dc into next 5 dc, 1 dc into next sp, 6 ch, miss next tr, 1 tr each into next 2 tr; rep from *, ss into 3rd ch.

17th rnd: 3 ch into ss, 1 tr into next tr, * (2 ch, 1 tr into next sp) 4 times, 2 ch, 1 tr 3 ch and 1 tr into next sp, (2 ch, 1 tr into next sp) 4 times, 2 ch, 1 tr each into next 2 tr, 8 ch, miss 1st dc, 1 dc each into next 5 dc, 8 ch, miss next dc, 1 tr each into next 2 tr; rep from *, ss into 3rd ch.

18th rnd: As for 17th rnd, but dec at dc and inc at 2 ch gps.

19th rnd: 3 ch into ss, 1 tr into next tr, * (2 ch, 1 tr into next sp) 6 times, 2 ch, 1 tr 3 ch and 1 tr into next sp, (2 ch, 1 tr into next sp) 6 times, 2 ch, 1 tr each into next 2 tr, 9 ch, 1 dc into centre of 3 dc, 9 ch, 1 tr each into next 2 tr; rep from *, ss into 3rd ch.

20th rnd: 3 ch into ss, 1 tr into next tr, * (2 ch, 1 tr into next sp) 7 times, 2 ch, 1 tr 3 ch and 1 tr into next sp, (2 ch, 1 tr into next sp) 7 times, 2 ch, 1 tr each into next 2 tr, 2 ch, 1 tr each into next 2 tr, rep from *, ss into 3rd ch.

21st rnd: 1 dc into ss, 3 ch, * 1 dc into next tr, 1 dc 3 ch and 1 dc into each sp to 2 tr, 1 dc into 1st tr, 3 ch and 1 dc into next tr, 1 dc 3 ch and 1 dc into next sp, 1 dc and 3 ch into tr; rep from *, ss into 1st dc.

Fasten off.

Pretty doily with leaves

(see photograph 1, p. 6)

MATERIALS: Approximately 40 g Madeira no. 5; crochet hook 1,75 mm

SIZE: 33 cm in diameter

Commence with 7 ch, join with ss to form a ring.

1st rnd: 12 dc into ring, ss into 1st dc.

2nd rnd: 1 dc into ss, * 5 ch, miss next dc, 1 dc into next dc; rep from *, ss into 1st dc (= 6 sps).

3rd rnd: ss across 2 ch and into centre of sp, 5 ch into ss (= 1 tr + 2 ch), 1 tr into same sp, * 5 ch, 1 tr 2 ch and 1 tr into next sp; rep from *, ss into 3rd of 5 ch.

4th rnd: ss into sp, 3 ch and 1 tr into sp, * 4 ch 1 dc and 4 ch into 5 ch sp, 2 tr into next sp; rep from *, ss into 3rd ch.

5th rnd: 3 ch and 1 tr into ss, * 2 tr into next tr, 5 ch, 1 unf tr into each of next 2 sps, yoh and draw through all lps, 5 ch, 2 tr into next tr; rep from *, ss into 3rd ch.

6th rnd: 3 ch and 1 tr into ss, * 1 tr each into next 2 tr, 2 tr into next tr, 5 ch, 1 unf tr into each of next 2 sps, yoh and draw through all lps, 5 ch, 2 tr into next tr; rep from *, ss into 3rd ch.

7th to 11th rnd: As 6th rnd, but inc 2 tr into each tr gp as before.

12th rnd: 3 ch into ss, * 1 tr each into next 4 tr, 5 ch, miss next 3 tr, 1 dc between next 2 tr, 5 ch, miss 3 tr, 1 tr into each of next 5 tr, 6 ch, 1 unf tr into each of next 2 sps, yoh and draw through all lps, 6 ch, 1 tr into next tr; rep from *, ss into 3rd ch.

13th rnd: 3 ch into ss, * 1 tr into each of next 4 tr, 6 ch, 1 unf tr into each of next 2 sps, 6 ch, 1 tr into each of next 5 tr, 5 ch, 1 unf tr into each of next 2 sps, 5 ch, 1 tr into next tr *, rep from * to *, ss into 3rd ch.

14th rnd: 3 ch into ss, * 1 tr into each of next 4 tr, 5 ch, 1 unf tr into each of next 2 sps, 5 ch, 1 tr into each of next 5 tr, 5 ch, 1 dc into sp, 5 ch, 1 dc into next sp, 5 ch, 1 tr into tr *, rep from * to *, ss into 3rd ch.

15th rnd: 3 ch into ss, * 1 tr into each of next 4 tr, 8 ch, 1 tr each into next 5 tr, 5 ch, 1 dc into sp, 5 ch, 1 tr 5 ch into next sp, 1 dc 5 ch into next sp, 1 tr into next tr; rep from *, ss into 3rd ch.

16th rnd: ss into tr, * 1 tr each into next 3 tr, 8 tr into 8 ch sp, 1 tr into each of next 4 tr, 6 ch, miss next tr, 1 dc into sp, 6 ch, 1 unf tr each into next 2 sps, 6 ch, 1 dc into next sp, 6 ch, miss next tr, 1 tr into next tr; rep from *, ss into 3rd ch.

17th rnd: ss into tr, 3 ch into ss, * 1 tr

Photograph 1: Pretty doily with leaves

each into next 13 tr, 8 ch, miss next tr, 1 unf tr each into next 2 sps, yoh and draw through all lps, 8 ch, (1 unf tr into same sp as previous unf tr, 1 unf tr into next sp, yoh and draw through all lps, 8 ch) twice, miss next tr, 1 tr into next tr; rep from *, ss into 3rd ch.

18th rnd: ss into tr, 3 ch into ss, * 1 tr

each into next 11 tr, 8 ch, miss next tr, 1 dc into sp, 8 ch, 1 unf tr into same sp, 1 unf tr into next sp, yoh and draw through all lps, 8 ch, (1 unf tr into same sp as last unf tr, 1 unf tr into next sp, yoh and draw through all lps, 8 ch) twice, 1 dc into same sp as last unf tr, 8 ch, miss next tr, 1 tr into next tr; rep from *, ss into 3rd ch.

19th t ways a 17th rn **22nd a** but om into sp ฯ ฯ ฯ thus no inc. **24th rnd:** ss into 8 ch sp, 7 dc into each sp all round, ss into 1st dc. Fasten off.

Granny square
(see photograph 2, p. 7)

MATERIALS: 30 g Madeira no. 5; crochet hook 1,75 mm

SIZE: 26 x 26 cm

Commence with 8 ch, ss into 1st ch to form a ring.
Please note: Unless otherwise instructed, replace first tr at beg of rnd with 3 ch.
1st rnd: 2 tr 3 ch and 2 tr into ring, (3 ch, 2 tr, 3 ch and 2 tr [= 1 open sh] into ring) 3 times, thus 4 open sh into ring.
2nd rnd: ss across tr into sp, open sh into open sh, * 2 ch, 3 tr into next sp, 2 ch, open sh into next open sh; rep from *, ss into 3rd ch.
3rd rnd: ss across tr and into sp, open sh into open sh, * (2 ch, 3 tr into next sp) twice, 2 ch, open sh into open sh; rep from *, ss into 3rd ch.
4th to 13th rnd: As 3rd rnd, inc as before.
14th rnd: 3 tr 3 ch and 3 tr into corner sp, 6 ch, miss next sp as well as 3 tr, * open sh into next sp, 6 ch, miss next gp of 3 tr 1 sp and 3 tr; rep from *, work remaining 3 corners as 1st, ss into 3rd ch.
15th rnd: ss across 2 tr and into sp, 4 tr 4 ch and 4 tr into sp, * 7 ch, open sh into open sh; rep from * working 4 tr 4 ch and 4 tr into each corner sp, ss into 3rd ch.
16th rnd: ss across 2 tr and into sp, 4 tr 4 ch and 4 tr into sp, * 5 ch, 2 dc around 2 lps from previous 2 rnds, 5

Photograph 2: Granny square

7

ch, open sh into open sh; rep from *, working 4 tr 4 ch and 4 tr into each corner sp, ss into 3rd ch.

17th rnd: ss across 3 tr and into sp, 5 tr 5 ch and 5 tr into sp, * 6 ch, 3 tr 3 ch and 3 tr into open sh; rep from *, working 5 tr 5 ch and 5 tr into each corner sp, ss into 3rd ch.

18th rnd: 1 dc into ss, 1 dc each into next 4 tr, 3 dc 4 ch and 3 dc into corner sp, 1 tr each into next 5 tr, 3 dc 4 ch and 3 dc into 6 ch sp, 1 dc each into next 3 tr, 1 dc 4 ch and 1 dc into tr sp, complete rnd, ss into 1st dc. Fasten off.

Flower motif
(see photograph 3, p. 9)

MATERIALS: Approximately 50 g Pingouin no. 8; crochet hook 1,25 mm

SIZE: 34 cm in diameter

Commence with 6 ch, join with ss to form a ring.

1st rnd: (1 dc and 3 ch into ring) 6 times, ss into 1st dc.

2nd rnd: ss into sp, 3 ch (= 1st tr) and 2 tr into same sp, * 3 ch, 3 tr into next sp; rep from *, ss into 3rd ch (= six 3 tr gps).

3rd rnd: 3 ch into ss, * 2 tr into next tr, 1 tr into next tr, 3 tr into sp, 1 tr into next tr; rep from *, ss into 3rd ch.

4th rnd: 7 ch and 1 tr into ss, * miss next 2 tr, 1 tr 4 ch and 1 tr into next tr; rep from *, ss into 3rd of 7 ch.

5th rnd: ss into sp, 3 ch and 3 tr into sp, * 3 ch and 4 tr into next sp; rep from *, ss into 3rd ch.

6th rnd: 3 ch into ss (= 1st tr), keeping last lp of each st on hook work 1 tr each into next 3 tr, yoh and draw through all lps on hook (= 4 tr cl), * 3 ch, 1 dc into 3 ch sp, 3 ch, 4 tr cl over 4 tr; rep from *, ss in top of first cl.

7th rnd: 13 ch into ss, * 1 tr in top of next cl, 10 ch; rep from *, ss into 3rd of 13 ch.

8th rnd: 1 dc into ss, * 8 dc into lp, 1 dc into next tr; rep from *, ss into 1st dc.

9th rnd: 1 dc into ss, * 3 ch, miss next dc, 1 dc into next dc; rep from *, ss into 1st dc.

10th rnd: ss to and into sp, 1 dc into same sp, * 3 ch, 1 dc into next sp; rep from *, ending with 1 ch, 1 htr into 1st dc.

11th to 12 rnd: 1 dc into lp made, complete as 10th rnd.

13th to 14th rnd: 1 dc into lp, * 4 ch, 1 dc into next sp; rep from *, ending with 2 ch, 1 htr into 1st dc.

15th rnd: 5 ch and 1 tr into lp, * 1 tr 2 ch and 1 tr into next sp; rep from *, ss into 3rd of 5 ch.

16th rnd: ss into 2 ch sp, 3 ch and 3 tr into sp, * 4 tr into next 2 ch sp; rep from *; ss into 3rd ch.

17th rnd: 3 ch into ss, * 1 tr each into next 11 tr, 4 ch, miss next tr, 1 dc each into next 2 tr, 4 ch, miss next tr, 1 tr each into next 12 tr, 2 ch, 1 tr into next tr; rep from *, ending with 2 ch, ss into 3rd ch.

18th rnd: 3 ch into ss, * 1 tr each into next 10 tr, 5 ch, miss next tr, 1 dc into dc, 5 ch, miss next tr, 1 tr each into next 11 tr, 2 ch, 1 tr into next tr; rep from *, ending with 2 ch, ss into 3rd ch.

19th rnd: 3 ch into ss, * 1 tr each into next 9 tr, 5 ch, miss next tr, 1 tr into dc, 5 ch, miss next tr, 1 tr each into next 10 tr, 2 ch, 1 tr into next tr; rep from *, ending with 2 ch, ss into 3rd ch.

20th rnd: 3 ch into ss, * 1 tr each into next 8 tr, 7 ch, miss next tr, 1 dc into dc, 7 ch, miss next tr, 1 tr each into next 9 tr, 2 ch, 1 tr into next tr; rep from *, ending with 2 ch, ss into 3rd ch.

21st rnd: 3 ch into ss, * 1 tr each into next 7 tr, 8 ch, miss next tr, 1 tr into dc, 8 ch, miss next tr, 1 tr each into next 8 tr, 2 ch, 1 tr into next tr; rep from *, ending with 2 ch, ss into 3rd ch.

22nd rnd: 3 ch into ss, * 1 tr each into next 6 tr, 9 ch, miss next tr, 1 dc into dc, 9 ch, miss next tr, 1 tr each into next 7 tr, 2 ch, 1 tr into next tr; rep from *, ending with 2 ch, ss into 3rd ch.

23rd rnd: 3 ch into ss, * 1 tr each into next 5 tr, 5 ch, miss next tr, 1 dc into 9 ch lp, 4 ch, 1 tr 3 ch and 1 tr into dc, 4 ch, 1 dc into next 9 ch lp, 5 ch, miss next tr, 1 tr each into next 6 tr, 1 ch, 1 tr into next tr; rep from *, ending with 1 ch, ss into 3rd ch.

24th rnd: 3 ch into ss, 1 tr each into next 4 tr, * 5 ch, miss next tr, 1 dc into next sp, 5 ch, 1 dc into next sp, 5 ch, 1 tr 3 ch and 1 tr into 3 ch sp, 5 ch, 1 dc into next sp, 5 ch, 1 dc into next sp, 5 ch, miss next tr, 1 tr each into next 10 tr; rep from *, ending with 5 tr, ss into 3rd ch.

25th rnd: 3 ch into ss, 1 tr each into next 3 tr, * 6 ch, miss next tr, (1 dc into next sp, 6 ch) 3 times, 1 tr 3 ch and 1 tr into 3 ch sp, 6 ch, (1 dc into next sp, 6 ch) 3 times, miss next tr, 1 tr each into next 8 tr; rep from *, ending with 4 tr, ss into 3rd ch.

26th to 27th rnd: As 25th rnd, but dec over tr gps as before.

28th rnd: ss across tr and next 2 ch, 1 dc into same sp, * (6 ch, 1 dc into next sp) 6 times, 6 ch, keeping last lp of each st on hook, work 2 tr into 3 ch sp, yoh and draw through all lps on hook (= 2 tr cl), 2 ch, work 2 more cls into same sp (= 3 cl and 2 sp in 3 ch sp), (6 ch, 1 dc into next sp) 6 times, 6 ch, miss 4 tr, 1 dc into next sp; rep from *, ending with 3 ch and 1 tr into 1st dc.

29th rnd: 1 dc in lp made, (7 ch, 1 dc into next sp) 6 times, * 7 ch, 1 cl into next 2 ch sp, 2 ch, 1 cl into next sp, (7 ch, 1 dc into next sp) 13 times; rep from *, ending with 3 ch and 1 dtr into 1st dc.

30th rnd: 4 ch into ss, 3 dc into same sp, (3 dc 4 ch and 3 dc into next sp) 7 times, * 3 ch, 1 cl between next 2 cl, 4 ch, ss into 1st ch (= p on top of cl), 3 ch, (3 dc 4 ch and 3 dc into next sp) 14 times; rep from *, ending with 3 dc, ss into 1st ch.
Fasten off.

Photograph 3: Flower motif

Pointed cloth

(see photograph 4, p. 10)

MATERIALS: Approximately 30 g Madeira no. 5; crochet hook 1,75 mm

SIZE: 20 cm in diameter

Commence with 12 ch, join with ss to form a ring.

1st rnd: 3 ch (= 1st tr) into ss, keeping last lps of each st on hook work 2 tr into ring, yoh and draw through all lps on hook (= one 3 tr cl), * 3 ch, 3 tr cl into ring; rep from * 7 times more, ss in top of 1st cl.

2nd rnd: ss into sp, 4 dc into each sp, ss into 1st dc.

3rd rnd: 1 dc into ss, * 4 ch, miss next dc, 1 dc into next dc; rep from *, ss into 1st dc.

4th rnd: ss into sp, 3 ch and 2 tr into same sp, 3 tr into next and every foll sp, ss into 3rd ch.

5th rnd: 1 dc into ss, * 5 ch, miss 2 tr, 1 dc into next tr; rep from *, ss into 1st dc.

6th rnd: ss into sp, 3 ch and 4 tr into same sp, 5 tr into next and every sp, ss into 3rd ch.

7th rnd: 1 dc into ss, * 7 ch, miss 4 tr, 1 dc into next tr; rep from *, ss into 1st dc.

8th rnd: ss into sp, 3 ch and 6 tr into same sp, 7 tr into next and every sp, ss into 3rd ch.

9th rnd: ss back into sp between tr gps, * 1 dc into same sp, 2 ch, miss 3 tr, 2 tr 3 ch and 2 tr into next tr (= open sh), 2 ch, miss next 3 tr, 1 dc into sp between tr gps; rep from *, ss into 1st dc.

10 rnd: 1 dc into ss, * 3 ch, open sh into open sh, 3 ch, 1 dc into dc; rep from *, ss into 1st dc.

11th rnd: 1 dc into ss, * 4 ch, open sh into open sh, 4 ch, 1 dc into dc; rep from *, ss into 1st dc.

12th rnd: 1 dc into ss, * 5 ch, open sh into open sh, 5 ch, 1 dc into dc; rep from *, ss into 1st dc.

13th rnd: 1 dc into ss, * 6 ch, 3 tr 3 ch and 3 tr for open sh, 6 ch, 1 dc into dc; rep from *, ss into 1st dc.

14th rnd: 1 dc into ss, * 7 ch, open sh into open sh, 7 ch, 1 dc into dc; rep from *, ss into 3rd ch. Fasten off.

Photograph 4: Pointed cloth

Photograph 5: Doily in chain stitch (left), small round doily (back) and easy to crochet (right)

Small round doily

(see photograph 5, p. 11)

MATERIALS: Approximately 30 g Pingouin no. 8; crochet hook 1,25 mm

SIZE: 19 cm in diameter

Commence with 10 ch, join with ss to form a ring.
1st rnd: 16 dc into ring, ss into 1st dc.
2nd rnd: 1 tr 1 ch into each dc (work 3 ch for 1st tr unless otherwise instructed), ss into 3rd ch.
3rd rnd: 1 tr 2 ch into each tr, ss into 3rd ch.

4th rnd: 1 tr 4 ch into each tr, ss into 3rd ch.
5th rnd: 1 tr 5 ch into each tr, ss into 3rd ch.
6th rnd: 1 tr into each tr and 5 tr into each sp, ss into 3rd ch.
7th rnd: 1 dc into ss, * 3 ch, miss 1 tr, 1 dc into next tr; rep from *, ss into 1st dc.
8th rnd: ss into sp, 2 tr 1 ch into each sp, ss into 3rd ch.
9th rnd: ss into sp, 1 dc 4 ch into each sp, ss into 1st dc.

10th rnd: ss into sp, 2 tr 2 ch into each sp, ss into 3rd ch.
11th rnd: ss into sp, 1 tr 3 ch into each sp, ss into 3rd ch.
12th rnd: 1 tr 4 ch into each tr, ss into 3rd ch.
13th and 14th rnd: 1 tr 5 ch into each tr, ss into 3rd ch.
15th rnd: As 6th rnd.
16th and 17th rnd: 1 tr into each tr, ss into 3rd ch. Fasten off.

Photograph 6: Doily with flared edge (back), doily with scalloped edging (left) and lily motif (front)

Doily with flared edge

(see photograph 6, p. 12)

MATERIALS: Approximately 30 g Madeira no. 5; crochet hook 1,75 mm

SIZE: 22 cm in diameter

Make 6 ch, join with ss to form a ring.
1st rnd: 10 dc into ring, ss into 1st dc.
2nd rnd: 2 dc into each dc, ss into 1st dc.
3rd rnd: 1 dc into each dc, ss into 1st dc.
4th rnd: 2 dc into ss, * miss next dc, 2 dc into next dc; rep from *, ss into 1st dc.
5th rnd: 4 ch into ss (= 1 tr and 1 ch), 1 tr 1 ch into each dc, ss into 3rd ch.

6th rnd: 5 ch into ss, 1 tr 2 ch into each tr, ss into 3rd ch.
7th rnd: 6 ch into ss, 1 tr 3 ch into each tr, ss into 3rd ch.
8th rnd: 7 ch into ss, 1 tr 4 ch into each tr, ss into 3rd ch.
9th rnd: 8 ch into ss, 1 tr 5 ch into each tr, ss into 3rd ch.
10th rnd: ss into sp, 3 ch into ss (= 1st tr), 4 tr into same sp, remove hook from lp and insert hook from front to back through ch at start, pick up lp and draw through (= 1 B), 5 ch, 1 B and 5 ch into each sp, ss into back and top of 1st B.
11th rnd: ss into sp, 1 B and 6 ch into

each sp, ss into back and top of 1st B.
12th rnd: ss into sp, 4 ch into ss (= 1 tr and 1 ch), (1 tr 1 ch) 3 times more into same sp, (1 tr 1 ch) 4 times into each sp, ss into 3rd of 4 ch.
13th rnd: 4 ch into ss, 1 tr 1 ch into each tr, ss into 3rd ch.
14th rnd: As 13th rnd.
15 rnd: 5 ch into ss, 1 tr 2 ch into each tr, ss into 3rd ch.
16th and 17th rnd: As 15th rnd.
18th rnd: ss into sp, 3 ch (= 1st tr), 3 tr into same sp, 1 B, (3 ch and 1 B) into each sp, ss in top of 1st B. Fasten off.

Lily motif

(see photograph 6, p. 12)

MATERIALS: Approximately 25 g Pingouin no. 8; crochet hook 1,75 mm

SIZE: 19 cm in diameter

Commence with 10 ch, join with ss to form a ring.
1st rnd: 3 ch (= 1st tr) into ss, 1 tr into ring, (2 ch 2 tr into ring) 7 times, 2 ch, ss into 3rd ch.
2nd rnd: ss across tr and into sp, 3 ch and 2 tr into sp, * 2 ch, 3 tr into next sp; rep from *, ss into 3rd ch.
3rd rnd: 3 ch into ss, 1 unf tr each into next 2 tr, yoh and draw through all lps on hook (= a 3 tr cl over 3 tr), * 3 ch 1 tr into sp, 3 ch, 1 cl over 3 tr; rep from *, ss in top of 1st cl.
4th rnd: ss across 3 ch and into tr, 3 ch and 2 tr into tr, * 8 ch, 3 tr into next tr; rep from *, ss into 3rd ch.
5th rnd: 3 ch into ss, 1 tr each into next 2 tr, * 4 ch, 2 tr into 8 ch sp, 4 ch, 1 tr each into next 3 tr; rep from *, ss into 3rd ch.
6th rnd: 3 ch into ss, 1 tr each into next 2 tr, * 4 ch, 2 tr each into next 2 tr (= 4 tr), 4 ch, 1 tr each into next 3 tr; rep from *, ss into 3rd ch.

7th rnd: 3 ch into ss, 1 tr each into next 2 tr, * 4 ch, 2 tr each into next 4 tr (= 8 tr), 4 ch, 1 tr each into next 3 tr; rep from *, ss into 3rd ch.
8th rnd: 3 ch into ss, 1 tr each into next 2 tr, * 3 ch, 2 tr into next tr, (1 ch 1 tr into each of next 2 tr) 3 times, 1 ch 2 tr into next tr (= 10 tr gps), 3 ch, 1 tr each into next 3 tr; rep from *, ss into 3rd ch.
9th rnd: 3 ch into ss, 1 tr each into next 2 tr, * 3 ch, (1 tr into next tr, 2 tr in next tr, 1 ch) 5 times, 3 ch, 1 tr each into next 3 tr; rep from *, ss into 3rd ch.
10th rnd: 3 ch into ss, 1 tr into each of next 2 tr, * 3 ch, (1 tr each into next 3 tr, 1 ch) 5 times, 3 ch, 1 tr each into next 3 tr; rep from *, ss into 3rd ch.
11th rnd: 3 ch into ss, 1 tr into each of next 2 tr, * 2 ch, (1 tr each into next 3 tr, 1 ch) 5 times, 2 ch, 1 tr each into next 3 tr; rep from *, ss into 3rd ch.
12th rnd: 3 ch into ss, 1 tr each into next 2 tr, * 1 ch, 1 tr each into next 3 tr; rep from *, ss into 3rd ch.
13th rnd: 3 ch into ss, 1 tr each into next 2 tr, * 5 ch, (miss 3 tr, 2 tr into next 1 ch sp, 3 ch) 4 times, 5 ch, miss

3 tr, 1 tr each into next 3 tr; rep from *, ss into 3rd ch.
14th rnd: 3 ch into ss, 1 tr each into next 2 tr, * 5 ch, (1 tr into next tr, 2 tr into next tr, 3 ch) 4 times, 5 ch, 1 tr each into next 3 tr; rep from *, ss into 3rd ch.
15 rnd: 3 ch into ss, 1 tr each into next 2 tr, * 5 ch, (1 tr into next tr, 2 tr into next tr, 1 tr into next tr, 3 ch) 4 times, 5 ch, 1 tr each into next 3 tr; rep from *, ss into 3rd ch.
16th rnd: 3 ch into ss, 1 tr each into next 2 tr, * 5 ch, (1 tr into tr, 2 tr into next tr, 1 tr each into next 2 tr, 3 ch) 4 times, 5 ch, 1 tr each into next 3 tr; rep from *, ss into 3rd ch.
17th rnd: 3 ch (= 1st tr) into ss, 1 unf tr each into next 2 tr, yoh and draw through all lps on hook, 4 ch, ss into 1st ch to form p (= 3 tr cl with p), *(8 ch, miss next 2 tr, 1 dc 4 ch and 1 dc into next tr) 4 times, 8 ch, 3 tr cl with p over next 3 tr; rep from *, ss in top of 1st cl. Fasten off.

Daisy

(see photograph 7, p. 14)

Photograph 7: Daisy

MATERIALS: Approximately 50 g Madeira no. 5; crochet hook 1,75 mm

SIZE: 32 cm in diameter

Make 8 ch, join with ss to form a ring.

1st rnd: 14 dc into ring, ss into 1st dc.

2nd rnd: 4 ch (= 1 tr and 1 ch) into ss, 1 tr 1 ch into each dc, ss into 3rd of 4 ch.

3rd rnd: ss into 1 ch sp, 3 ch and 1 tr into sp, 2 tr 2 ch into each 1 ch sp, ss into 3rd ch.

4th rnd: ss across 1 tr and into sp, 3 ch and 2 tr into same sp, * 2 ch, 3 tr into next sp; rep from *, ss into 3rd ch.

5th rnd: ss across 2 tr and into sp, 3 ch and 3 tr into same sp, * 2 ch, 4 tr into next sp; rep from *, ss into 3rd ch.

6th rnd: 3 ch into ss, 1 tr into tr, * 2 ch, 1 tr into each of next 2 tr, 2 ch, 1 tr each into next 2 tr; rep from *, ss into 3rd ch.

7th rnd: 3 ch into ss, * 2 tr into next tr, 2 ch, 2 tr into next tr, 1 tr into next tr, 2 ch, 1 tr into next tr; rep from *, ss into 3rd ch.

8th rnd: ss into tr, 3 ch into ss, * 1 tr into next tr, 2 ch, 1 tr each into next 2 tr, 3 ch, miss next tr, 1 tr into next tr, 2 tr into next tr, 1 tr into next tr, 2 ch, 1 tr into next tr, 2 tr into next tr, 1 tr into next tr, 3 ch, miss next tr; rep from *, ss into 3rd ch.

9th rnd: 3 ch into ss, 1 tr each into next 3 tr, * 3 ch 1 tr into each of next 3 tr, 2 tr into next tr, 2 ch, 2 tr into next tr, 1 tr each into next 3 tr, 3 ch, 1 tr each into next 4 tr; rep from *, ss into 3rd ch.

10th rnd: 3 ch into ss, keeping last lp of each tr on hook work 1 tr each into next 3 tr, yoh and draw through all lps on hook (= one 4 tr cl), * 4 ch, 1 tr in each of next 4 tr, 2 tr into next tr, 2 ch, 2 tr into next tr, 1 tr each into next 4 tr, 4 ch, 1 cl over next 4 tr; rep from *, ss in top of 1st cl.

11th rnd: ss across 4 ch and into tr, 3 ch into ss, * 1 tr into each of next 4 tr, 2 tr into next tr, 2 ch, 2 tr into next tr, 1 tr into each of next 5 tr, 8 ch, miss cl, 1 tr into next tr; rep from *, ss into 3rd ch.

12th rnd: 3 ch into ss, * 1 tr each into next 5 tr, 2 tr into next tr, 2 ch, 2 tr into next tr, 1 tr each into next 6 tr, 4 ch, 1 dc into 8 ch sp, 4 ch, 1 tr into next tr; rep from *, ss into 3rd ch.

13th rnd: 3 ch into ss, * 1 tr each into next 6 tr, 2 tr into next tr, 2 ch, 2 tr into next tr, 1 tr each into next 7 tr, 5 ch, 1 dc into dc, 5 ch, 1 tr into next tr; rep from *, ss into 3rd ch.

14th rnd: 3 ch into ss, * 1 tr each into next 7 tr, 2 tr into next tr, 2 ch, 2 tr into next tr, 1 tr each into next 8 tr, 6 ch, 1 dc into dc, 6 ch, 1 tr into next tr; rep from *, ss into 3rd ch.

15 rnd: 3 ch into ss, * 1 tr each into next 8 tr, 2 tr into next tr, 2 ch, 2 tr into next tr, 1 tr each into next 9 tr, 10 ch, 1 tr into next tr; rep from *, ss into 3rd ch.

16th rnd: 3 ch into ss, * 1 tr each into next 9 tr, 2 tr into next tr, 2 ch, 2 tr into next tr, 1 tr each into next 10 tr, 5 ch, 1 dc into 10 ch sp, 5 ch, 1 tr into next tr; rep from *, ss into 3rd ch.

17th rnd: 3 ch into ss, * 1 tr into each of next 10 tr, 2 tr into next tr, 2 ch and 2 tr into next tr, 1 tr into each of next 11 tr, 6 ch, 1 dc into dc, 6 ch, 1 tr into next tr; rep from *, ss into 3rd ch.

18th rnd: 3 ch into ss, * 1 tr into each of next 11 tr, 2 tr into next tr, 2 ch, 2 tr into next tr, 1 tr each into next 12 tr, 7 ch, 1 dc into dc, 7 ch, 1 tr into next tr; rep from *, ss into 3rd ch.

19th rnd: 3 ch into ss, * 1 tr into each of next 12 tr, 2 tr into next tr, 2 ch, 2 tr into next tr, 10 ch, ss into 6th ch from hook to form a ring, 4 ch, 1 tr into next tr; rep from *, ss into 3rd ch.

20th rnd: ss across next tr and into 3rd tr, 3 ch into ss, * 1 tr into each of next 11 tr, 6 ch, miss next 2 tr, 4 tr into ring made in previous rnd, 6 ch, miss next 2 tr, 1 tr into next tr; rep from *, ss into 3rd ch.

21st rnd: ss across next tr and into 3rd tr, 3 ch into ss, * 1 tr each into next 11 tr, 3 ch, 1 tr each into next 12 tr, 6 ch, miss next 2 tr, 2 tr into each of next 4 tr, 6 ch, miss next 2 tr, 1 tr into next tr; rep from *, ss into 3rd ch.

22nd rnd: ss across tr and into 3rd tr, 3 ch into ss, * 1 tr into each of next 9 tr, 3 ch, 1 tr into each of next 10 tr, 6 ch, miss next 2 tr, 1 tr and 1 ch into each of foll 8 tr, 6 ch, miss 2 tr, 1 tr into next tr; rep from *, ss into 3rd ch.

23rd rnd: ss across tr and into 3rd tr, 3 ch into ss, * 1 tr each into next 7 tr, 4 ch, 1 tr into each of foll 8 tr, 6 ch, miss 2 tr, 1 tr and 2 ch into each of next 8 tr, 6 ch, miss 2 tr, 1 tr into next tr; rep from *, ss into 3rd ch.

24th rnd: ss across tr and into 3rd tr, 3 ch into ss, * 1 tr into each of next 5 tr, 5 tr into 4 ch sp, 1 tr each into next 6 tr, 7 ch, miss next 2 tr, (1 tr into tr, 2 tr into 2 ch sp) 7 times, 7 ch, miss next 2 tr, 1 tr into next tr; rep from *, ss into 3rd ch. Fasten off.

Easy to crochet

(see photograph 5, p. 11)

MATERIALS: Approximately 30 g Madeira no. 5; crochet hook 1,75 mm

SIZE: 22 cm in diameter

Commence with 6 ch, join with ss to form a ring.

1st rnd: 3 ch (= 1st tr) into ss, 2 unf tr into ring, yoh and draw through all lps on hook (= 3 tr cl), (3 ch, 1 cl into ring) 5 times, ss in top of 1st cl.

2nd rnd: 1 dc into ss, * 4 ch, 1 dc into sp, 4 ch, 1 dc in top of cl; rep from *, ending with 2 ch and 1 htr into 1st dc (= 12 sps).

3rd rnd: 1 dc into lp made, 4 ch 1 dc into each sp, ss into 1st dc.

4th rnd: ss into sp, 4 tr cl into same sp, 5 ch and 1 cl into next and every foll sp, ss in top of 1st cl.

5th rnd: ss across 2 ch and into sp, 1 dc into same sp, * 6 ch, 1 dc into next sp; rep from *, ss into 1st dc.

6th rnd: ss into sp, 3 ch into ss, 5 tr into same sp, * 2 ch 6 tr into next sp; rep from *, ss into 3rd ch.

7th rnd: ss into tr, 3 ch into ss, * 1 tr each into next 4 tr, 2 ch, 1 tr each into next 5 tr, 5 ch, miss next 2 tr, 1 tr into next tr; rep from *, ss into 3rd ch.

8th rnd: ss into tr, 3 ch into ss, * 1 tr into each of next 3 tr, 2 ch, 1 tr each into next 4 tr, 4 ch, miss next tr, 1 dc into sp, 4 ch, miss next tr, 1 tr into next tr; rep from *, ss into 3rd ch.

9th rnd: ss into tr, 3 ch into ss, * 1 tr each into next 2 tr, 2 ch, 1 tr each into next 3 tr, 5 ch, miss next tr, 1 dc into next sp, 5 ch, 1 dc into next sp, 5 ch, miss next tr, 1 tr into next tr; rep from *, ss into 3rd ch.

10th rnd: ss into tr, 3 ch into ss, * 1 tr into next tr, 2 tr into sp, 1 tr each into next 2 tr, 5 ch, miss next tr, 1 dc 5 ch into each of next 3 sps, miss next tr, 1 tr into next tr; rep from *, ss into 3rd ch.

11th rnd: ss into tr, 3 ch into ss, * 1 tr each into next 3 tr, 6 ch, miss next tr, 1 dc 6 ch into each of next 4 sps, miss next tr, 1 tr into next tr; rep from *, ss into 3rd ch.

12th rnd: ss into tr, * 1 tr into next tr, 6 ch, miss next tr, 1 dc into next sp, 6 ch, 1 dc into next sp, 6 ch, 6 tr into next sp, 6 ch, 1 dc into next sp, 6 ch 1 dc into next sp, 6 ch, miss next tr, 1 tr into next tr; rep from *, ending with 3 ch and 1 tr into 3rd ch.

13th rnd: 1 dc into lp just made, 6 ch 1 dc into each of next 3 sps, * 4 ch, miss next tr, 1 tr each into next 4 tr, 4 ch, miss next tr, 1 dc into next sp, 6 ch, 1 dc into each of next 5 sps; rep from *, ending with 3 ch and 1 tr into 1st dc.

14th rnd: 1 dc into lp just made, 6 ch 1 dc into each of next 4 sps, * 4 ch, miss next tr, 1 tr each into next 2 tr, 4 ch, miss next tr, 1 dc into next sp, 6 ch 1 dc into each of next 6 sps; rep from *, ending with 3 ch and 1 tr into 1st dc.

15th and 16th rnd: 1 dc into lp just made, 6 ch 1 dc into each sp, ending with 3 ch, and 1 tr into 1st dc.

17th rnd: 1 dc into lp, 7 ch 1 dc into each sp, ss into 1st dc.

18th rnd: 4 dc 4 ch and 4 dc into each sp, ss into 1st dc. Fasten off.

Doily with scalloped edging

(see photograph 6, p. 12)

MATERIALS: Approximately 30 g Pingouin no. 8; crochet hook 1,25 mm

SIZE: 18 cm in diameter

Make 6 ch, join with ss to form a ring.

1st rnd: 3 ch (= 1st tr), 16 tr into ring (= 17 tr).

2nd rnd: 3 ch and 1 tr into ss, 2 tr into each tr, ss into 3rd ch.

3rd rnd: 4 ch into ss, 1 tr 1 ch into each tr, ss into 3rd of 4 ch.

4th rnd: ss into 1 ch sp, 3 ch (= 1 tr), keeping last lp of each st on hook work 2 tr into same sp, yoh and draw through all lps on hook (= 3 tr cl), * 5 ch, miss next 1 ch sp, 3 tr cl into next sp; rep from *, ss in top of 1st cl.

5th rnd: ss into sp, 5 dc into sp, * 2 ch, 5 dc into next sp; rep from *, ending with 2 ch and ss into 1st dc.

6th rnd: ss across next 4 dc and into 2 ch sp, 3 ch (= 1 tr), 3 tr into same sp, * 3 ch, 4 tr into next 2 ch sp; rep from *, ss into 3rd ch.

7th rnd: 3 ch into ss, 1 tr each into next 3 tr, * 3 ch, 1 tr each into next 4 tr; rep from *, ss into 3rd ch.

8th rnd: As 7th rnd.

9th rnd: 3 ch into ss, 1 tr each into next 3 tr, * 3 ch, 1 dc and 3 ch into 3 ch sp, 1 tr each into next 4 tr; rep from *, ss into 3rd ch.

10th rnd: 3 ch into ss, 1 tr each into next 3 tr, * 5 ch, 1 tr each into next 4 tr; rep from *, ss into 3rd ch.

11th rnd: 3 ch into ss, 1 tr each into next 3 tr, * 3 ch, 1 dc and 3 ch into 5 ch sp, 1 tr each into next 4 tr; rep from *, ss into 3rd ch.

12th rnd: As 10th rnd, but work 7 ch between tr gps.

13th rnd: 3 ch into ss, 1 tr each into next 3 tr, * 4 ch 1 dc and 4 ch into 7 ch sp, 1 tr each into next 4 tr; rep from *, ss into 3rd ch.

14th rnd: As 12th rnd, but work 9 ch between tr gps.

15th rnd: 3 ch into ss, 1 tr each into next 3 tr, * 5 ch 1 dc and 5 ch into 9 ch sp, 1 tr each into next 4 tr; rep from *, ss into 3rd ch.

16th rnd: As 14th rnd, but work 11 ch between tr gps.

17th rnd: 1 dc into ss, 4 ch, * miss next 2 tr, 1 dc into next tr, (4 ch 1 dc) twice into 11 ch sp, 4 ch, 1 dc into tr, 4 ch; rep from *, ss into 1st dc.

18th rnd: ss into sp, 3 ch for 1st tr, 2 tr 3 ch and 3 tr into same sp, * 1 ch, 1 tr into next sp, 1 ch, 3 tr 3 ch and 3 tr into next sp; rep from *, ending with 1 ch and 1 tr into last sp, 1 ch, ss into 3rd ch. Fasten off.

Doily in chain stitch

(see photograph 5, p. 11)

MATERIALS: Approximately 25 g Madeira no. 5; crochet hook 1,75 mm

SIZE: 22 cm in diameter

Commence with 7 ch, join with ss to form a ring.

1st rnd: 16 dc into ring, ss into 1st dc.

2nd rnd: 1 dc into ss, * 3 ch, miss next dc, 1 dc into next dc; rep from *, ending with 1 dc and 1 htr into 1st dc.

3rd rnd: 1 dc into lp just made, * 5 ch, 1 dc into sp; rep from *, ss into 1st dc.

4th rnd: ss into sp, 3 ch into ss (= 1st tr), 5 tr into same sp, * 1 ch, 6 tr into next sp; rep from *, ss into 3rd ch.

5th rnd: Turn work to face wrong side, ss into 1 ch sp, turn work around and make 10 ch into ss (= 1 tr + 7 ch), * miss 6 tr, 1 tr into next 1 ch sp, 7 ch; rep from *, ss into 3rd of 10 ch.

6th rnd: ss into sp, 3 ch into ss, 7 tr into same sp, * 1 ch, 8 tr into next sp; rep from *, ss into 3rd ch.

7th rnd: Turn work to face wrong side and ss into 1 ch sp, turn back, make 13 ch into ss (= 1 tr + 10 ch), * miss 8 tr, 1 tr into next 1 ch sp, 10 ch; rep from *, ss into 3rd of 13 ch.

8th rnd: ss into sp, 3 ch into ss, 10 tr into same sp, * 2 ch, 11 tr into next sp; rep from *, ss into 3rd ch.

9th rnd: 1 dc into ss, * 3 ch, miss next tr, 1 dc into next tr; rep from *, ending with 1 ch and 1 htr into 1st dc.

10th rnd: 1 dc into lp made, * 4 ch, 1 dc into next sp; rep from *, ending with 2 ch and 1 tr into 1st dc.

11th to 17th rnd: As 10th rnd.

18th to 19th rnd: 1 dc in lp made, * 5 ch, 1 dc into next sp; rep from *, ending with 2 ch and 1 tr into 1st dc.

20th rnd: As 19th rnd, but work 6 ch and end with 3 ch and 1 tr into 1st dc.

21st rnd: As 20th rnd, but end with ss into 1st dc.

22nd rnd: 3 dc 4 ch and 3 dc into each sp, ss into 1st dc. Fasten off.

Doily with centre star

(see photograph 8, p. 17)

MATERIALS: Approximately 50 g Pingouin no. 8; crochet hook 1,25 mm

SIZE: 37 cm in diameter

Commence with 10 ch, join with ss to form a ring.

1st rnd: 3 ch (= 1st tr) into ss, 2 tr into ring, (1 ch 3 tr into ring) 6 times (= seven 3 tr gps), ss into 3rd ch.

2nd rnd: 3 ch and 1 tr into ss, * 1 tr into next tr, 2 tr into next tr, 1 ch 2 tr into next tr; rep from *, ss into 3rd ch.

3rd rnd: 3 ch and 1 tr into ss, * 1 tr each into next 3 tr, 2 tr into next tr, 1 ch, 2 tr into next tr; rep from *, ss into 3rd ch.

4th rnd: 3 ch and 1 tr into ss, * 1 tr into each of next 5 tr, 2 tr into next tr, 2 ch, 2 tr into next tr; rep from *, ss into 3rd ch.

5th rnd: 3 ch and 1 tr into ss, * 1 tr each into next 7 tr, 2 tr into next tr, 2 ch, 2 tr into next tr; rep from *, ss into 3rd ch.

6th rnd: 3 ch and 1 tr into ss, * 1 tr each into next 9 tr, 2 tr into next tr, 3 ch, 2 tr into next tr; rep from *, ss into 3rd ch.

7th rnd: 3 ch and 1 tr into ss, * 1 tr each into next 11 tr, 2 tr into next tr, 4 ch, 2 tr into next tr; rep from *, ss into 3rd ch.

8th rnd: 3 ch and 1 tr into ss, * 1 tr each into next 13 tr, 2 tr into next tr, 5 ch, 2 tr into next tr; rep from *, ss into 3rd ch.

9th rnd: ss into 2nd tr, 3 ch into ss (= 1st tr), * 1 tr each into next 14 tr, 2 ch, miss next tr, 3 tr into 5 ch sp, 2 ch, miss next tr, 1 tr into next tr; rep from *, ss into 3rd ch.

10th rnd: ss into 2nd tr, 3 ch, * 1 tr each into next 12 tr, 2 ch, miss next tr, 3 tr into sp, 3 ch, miss 3 tr, 3 tr into next sp, 2 ch, miss next tr, 1 tr into next tr; rep from *, ss into 3rd ch.

11th rnd: ss into 2nd tr, 3 ch into ss, * 1 tr into each of next 10 tr, 2 ch, miss next tr, (3 tr into sp, 3 ch) twice, 3 tr into next sp, 2 ch, miss next tr, 1 tr into next tr; rep from *, ss into 3rd ch.

12th to 15th rnd: Work as for previous rnds; in 15th rnd there should be a 3 tr gp at top with 7 filled squares between points.

16th rnd: Turn work to face wrong side, ss into 2 ch sp, turn back, 6 ch into ss, miss 3 tr, (3 tr into next sp, 3 ch) 3 times, 3 tr into next sp, * 2 ch, 2 tr into next tr, 1 tr into next tr, 2 tr into next tr, 2 ch, (3 tr into next sp, 3 ch) 7 times, 3 tr into sp; rep from *, ending with 2 tr into last sp, ss into 3rd of 6 ch.

17th rnd: ss into sp, 3 ch into ss (= 1st tr), 2 tr into same sp, (3 ch 3 tr into next sp) 3 times, * 3 ch, miss next 3 tr, 2 tr into next tr, 1 tr each into next 3 tr, 2 tr into next tr, (3 ch, miss next 3 tr, 3 tr into next sp) 7 times; rep from *, ss into 3rd ch.

18th rnd: Turn work to face wrong side, ss into sp, turn back, 6 ch into ss, (3 tr into next sp, 3 ch) 3 times, 3 tr into next sp, * 2 ch, 2 tr into next tr, 1 tr into each of next 5 tr, 2 tr into next tr, 2 ch, (3 tr into next sp, 3 ch) 7 times, 3 tr into next sp; rep from *, ending with 2 tr into last sp, ss into 3rd of 6 ch.

Photograph 8: Doily with centre star

19th rnd: ss into sp, 3 ch into ss (= 1st tr), 2 tr into same sp, (3 ch 3 tr into next sp) 3 times, * 3 ch, 2 tr into next tr, 1 tr into each of next 7 tr, 2 tr into next tr, (3 ch, miss next 3 tr, 3 tr into next sp) 7 times; rep from *, ss into 3rd ch.

20th rnd: Turn work to face wrong side, ss into sp, turn back, 6 ch into ss, (3 tr into next sp, 3 ch) 3 times, 3 tr into next sp, * 2 ch, miss next tr, 1 tr each into next 9 tr, 2 ch, miss next tr, (3 tr into next sp, 3 ch) 7 times, 3 tr into next sp; rep from *, ending with 2 tr into last sp, ss into 3rd of 6 ch.

21st rnd: ss into sp, 3 ch in ss (= 1st tr), 2 tr into same sp, (3 ch, 3 tr into next sp) 4 times, * 2 ch, miss next tr, 1 tr into each of next 7 tr, 2 ch, miss next tr, (3 tr into next sp, 3 ch) 8 times, 3 tr into next sp; rep from *, ss into 3rd ch.

22nd rnd: Turn work to face wrong side, ss into sp, turn back, 6 ch into

sp, (3 tr into next sp, 3 ch) 4 times, 3 tr into next sp, * 2 ch, miss next tr, 1 tr into each of next 5 tr, 2 ch, miss next tr, (3 tr 3 ch into next sp) 9 times, 3 tr into next sp, rep from *, ending with 2 tr into last sp, ss into 3rd of 6 ch.

23rd rnd: ss into sp, 3 tr into ss (= 1st tr), 2 tr into same sp, (3 ch, 3 tr into next sp) 5 times, * 2 ch, miss next tr, 1 tr into each of next 3 tr, 2 ch, miss next tr, (3 tr 3 ch into next sp) 10 times, 3 tr into next sp, rep from *, ss into 3rd ch.

24th rnd: Turn work to face wrong side, ss into sp, turn back, 6 ch into ss, * 3 tr into next sp, 3 ch; rep from *, ending with 2 tr into last sp, ss into 3rd of 6 ch.

25th rnd: ss into sp, 3 ch into ss (= 1st tr), 1 tr 3 ch and 2 tr into same sp, * 8 ch, miss 3 tr 1 sp and 3 tr, 2 tr 3 ch and 2 tr into next sp; rep from *, ss into 3rd ch.

26th rnd: ss across tr and into sp, 3

ch, 1 tr 3 ch and 2 tr into same sp, * 8 ch, 2 tr 3 ch and 2 tr into next 3 ch sp; rep from *, ss into 3rd ch.

27th rnd: ss across tr and into sp, 3 ch 1 tr 3 ch and 2 tr into same sp, * 5 ch, 2 dc around two 8 ch sps of previous 2 rnds, 5 ch, 2 tr 3 ch and 2 tr into next 3 ch sp; rep from *, ss into 3rd ch.

28th rnd: ss across tr and into sp, 3 ch 2 tr 3 ch and 3 tr into same sp, * 8 ch, 3 tr 3 ch and 3 tr into next 3 ch sp; rep from *, ss into 3rd ch.

29th rnd: 1 dc into ss, * 1 dc 4 ch into next tr, ss into 1st ch to form p on dc, 1 dc into next tr, 1 dc into sp, 1 dc with p and 1 dc into same sp, 1 dc into next tr, 1 dc with p into next tr, 1 dc into last tr, 3 dc into 8 ch sp, 1 dc with p and 4 dc into same sp, 1 dc into next tr; rep from *, ss into 3rd ch. Fasten off.

Photograph 9: Pineapple motif

Pineapple motif

(see photograph 9, p. 18)

MATERIALS: Approximately 50 g Madeira no. 5; crochet hook 1,75 mm

SIZE: 35 cm in diameter

Commence with 7 ch, join with ss to form a ring.

1st rnd: 5 ch into ss (= 1 tr and 2 ch), (1 tr 2 ch into ring) 10 times, ss into 3rd of 5 ch (= 12 tr in ring).

2nd rnd: ss into sp, 3 ch (= 1st tr), 1 tr 3 ch and 2 tr into same sp, * 2 ch, miss next sp, 2 tr 3 ch and 2 tr (= open sh) into next sp; rep from *, ss into 3rd ch.

3rd rnd: ss into open sh, * open sh into open sh, 4 ch; rep from *, ss into 1st dc.

4th rnd: ss into open sh, open sh into open sh, * 3 ch 1 tr into 4 ch sp, 3 ch, open sh into open sh; rep from *, ss into 3rd ch.

5th rnd: ss into open sh, * open sh into open sh, 3 ch, 1 tr 3 ch and 1 tr into next tr, 3 ch; rep from *, ss into 3rd ch.

6th rnd: ss into open sh, * open sh into open sh, 4 ch, 1 dc into next tr, 3 ch, 1 tr 3 ch and 1 tr into next ch sp, 3 ch, 1 dc into next tr, 4 ch; rep from *, ss into 3rd ch.

7th rnd: ss into open sh, * (2 tr 2 ch) 3 times into open sh, 6 ch, miss 2 sps, 1 tr 3 ch and 1 tr into next sp, 6 ch; rep from *, ss into 3rd ch.

8th rnd: ss into 2 ch sp, * open sh into sp, 2 ch, open sh into next sp, 3 ch 1 dc and 3 ch into 6 ch sp, 1 dc into tr, 3 ch, 1 tr 3 ch and 1 tr into next sp, 3 ch, 1 dc into tr, 3 ch 1 dc and 3 ch into 6 ch sp; rep from *, ss into 3rd ch.

9th rnd: ss into open sh, * open sh into open sh, 3 ch, open sh into next open sh, 6 ch, miss next three 3 ch sp, 1 tr 3 ch and 1 tr into next 3 ch sp, 6 ch; rep from *, ss into 3rd ch.

10th rnd: ss into open sh, * open sh into open sh, 2 ch 3 tr and 2 ch into 3 ch sp, open sh into open sh, 3 ch 1 dc and 3 ch into 6 ch sp, 1 dc into tr, 3 ch, 1 tr 3 ch and 1 tr into next sp, 3 ch, 1 dc into tr, 3 ch 1 dc and 3 ch into 6 ch sp; rep from *, ss into 3rd ch.

11th rnd: ss into open sh, * open sh into open sh, 2 ch, 1 tr into tr, 2 tr into next tr, 1 tr into tr, 2 ch, open sh into open sh, 6 ch, miss three 3 ch sp, 1 tr 3 ch and 1 tr into next sp, 6 ch; rep from *, ss into 3rd ch.

12th rnd: ss into open sh, * open sh into open sh, 2 ch, 1 tr into tr, 2 tr into next tr, 1 tr into each of next 2 tr, 2 ch, open sh into open sh, 3 ch 1 dc and 3 ch into 6 ch sp, 1 dc into tr, 3 ch, 1 tr 3 ch and 1 tr into next sp, 3 ch 1 dc into tr, 3 ch 1 dc and 3 ch into 6 ch sp; rep from *, ss into 3rd ch.

13th rnd: ss into open sh, * open sh into open sh, 2 ch, 1 tr into each of next 2 tr, 2 tr into next tr, 1 tr each into next 2 tr, 2 ch, open sh into open sh, 6 ch, miss three 3 ch sp, 1 tr 3 ch and 1 tr into next sp, 6 ch; rep from *, ss into 3rd ch.

14th rnd: ss into open sh, * open sh into open sh, 2 ch, 1 tr into tr, 2 tr into next tr, 1 tr each into next 4 tr, 2 ch, open sh into open sh, 3 ch 1 dc and 3 ch into 6 ch sp, 1 dc into tr, 3 ch, 1 tr 3 ch and 1 tr into next sp, 3 ch, 1 dc into tr, 3 ch 1 dc and 3 ch into 6 ch sp; rep from *, ss into 3rd ch.

15th rnd: ss into open sh, 3 ch 1 tr * 2 ch 2 tr 2 ch and 2 tr into open sh, 2 ch, 2 tr into next tr, 1 tr each into next 5 tr, 2 tr into next tr, 2 ch, 2 tr 2 ch and 2 tr into next open sh, 6 ch, 7 tr into 3 ch sp, 6 ch, 2 tr; rep from *, ss into 3rd ch.

16th rnd: ss into sp, * open sh into sp, 2 ch, open sh into next sp, 2 ch, miss next tr, 1 tr each into next 7 tr, 2 ch, miss next tr, open sh into next sp, 2 ch, open sh into next sp, 5 ch, 1 tr 1 ch into each of next 7 tr, 5 ch; rep from *, ss into 3rd ch.

17th rnd: ss into open sh, * open sh into open sh, 4 ch, open sh into next open sh, 2 ch, miss next tr, 1 tr each into next 5 tr, 2 ch, miss next tr, open sh into open sh, 4 ch, open sh into open sh, 4 ch, 1 tr 1 ch into each of next six 1 ch sps, 4 ch; rep from *, ss into 3rd ch.

18th rnd: ss into open sh, * open sh into open sh, 5 ch, open sh into next open sh, 2 ch, miss next tr, 1 tr each into next 3 tr, 2 ch, open sh into open sh, 5 ch, open sh into open sh, 4 ch, 1 tr 1 ch into each of next five 1 ch sps, 4 ch; rep from *, ss into 3rd ch.

19th rnd: ss into open sh, * open sh into open sh, 7 ch, open sh into open sh, 2 ch, 1 tr into centre of 3 tr, 2 ch, open sh into next open sh, 7 ch, open sh into next open sh, 5 ch, 1 tr 1 ch into each of next four 1 ch sps, 5 ch; rep from *, ss into 3rd ch.

20th rnd: ss into open sh, * open sh into open sh, 3 ch, 1 tr 3 ch and 1 tr into 7 ch sp, 3 ch, open sh into open sh, 1 ch, open sh into next open sh, 3 ch, 1 tr 3 ch and 1 tr into 7 ch sp, open sh into open sh, 6 ch, 1 tr 1 ch into each of next three 1 ch sp, 6 ch; rep from *, ss into 3rd ch.

21st rnd: ss into open sh, * open sh into open sh, 2 ch, 7 tr into 3 ch sp, 2 ch, open sh into open sh, open sh into next open sh, 2 ch, 7 tr into 3 ch sp, 2 ch, open sh into next open sh, 6 ch, 1 tr 1 ch into 1 ch sp, 1 tr into next 1 ch sp, 6 ch; rep from *, ss into 3rd ch.

22nd rnd: ss into open sh, * open sh into open sh, 2 ch, 1 tr 1 ch into each of next 7 tr, 2 ch, open sh into open sh, 2 ch, open sh into next open sh, 2 ch, 1 tr 1 ch into each of next 7 tr, 2 ch, open sh into open sh, 4 ch, 3 unf tr into next 1 ch sp, yoh and draw through all lps on hook, 4 ch, ss into 1st ch, (= 1 tr and 1 p on cl), 2 ch, 1 cl 1 p into same sp, 4 ch; rep from *, ss into 3rd ch.

23rd rnd: ss into open sh, * (1 cl 1 p and 2 ch) 3 times into same open sh, (1 dc 1 p into next tr, 1 ch, 1 dc into next tr) 4 times, 2 ch, (1 cl 1 p and 2 ch) 3 times into each open sh, 2 ch, (1 dc 1 p into next tr, 1 ch, 1 dc into next tr) 4 times, 2 ch, (1 cl 1 p and 2 ch) 3 times into open sh, 3 ch, 1 cl 1 p between next 2 cl, 3 ch; rep from *, ss into 1st tr. Fasten off.

Photograph 10: Small square cloth

Small square cloth
(see photograph 10, p. 20)

MATERIALS: Approximately 30 g Pingouin no. 8; crochet hook 1,25 mm

SIZE: 22 x 22 cm

Commence with 10 ch, join with ss to form a ring.

1st rnd: 3 ch (= 1st tr), 2 tr into ring but keep last lp of each st on hook, yoh and draw through all lps on hook (= 3 tr cl), 3 ch, (3 tr cl 3 ch) 7 times, ss in top of 1st cl.

2nd rnd: ss to and into 3 ch sp, 3 ch into ss, 1 tr 3 ch and 2 tr into same sp, * 2 tr 3 ch and 2 tr into next sp (= open sh); rep from *, ss into 3rd ch.

3rd rnd: ss across tr and into sp, 3 ch (= 1st tr), open sh into open sh, * 4 ch, open sh into next open sh; rep from *, ss into 3rd ch.

4th rnd: ss across tr and into sp, * open sh into open sh, 5 ch, 8 tr into next open sh, 5 ch; rep from *, ss into 3rd ch.

5th rnd: ss across tr and into sp, open sh into open sh, * 5 ch, 1 tr 1 ch into each of next 8 tr, 5 ch, open sh into next open sh; rep from *, ss into 3rd ch.

6th rnd: ss across tr and into sp, open sh into open sh, * 5 ch, 1 dc 2 ch into each of next 8 tr, 5 ch, open sh into next open sh; rep from *, ss into 3rd ch.

7th rnd: ss across tr and into sp, open sh into open sh, * 6 ch, 1 open sh into first 2 ch sp, 3 ch, miss next 2 sp, 1 open sh into next sp, 3 ch, miss next 2 sp, 1 open sh into last sp, 6 ch, open sh into next open sh; rep from *, ss into 3rd ch.

8th rnd: ss across tr and into sp, open sh into open sh, * 7 ch, open sh into next open sh, 2 ch, 1 dc into 3 ch sp, 2 ch, open sh into open sh, 2 ch, 1 dc into next sp, 2 ch, open sh into next open sh, 7 ch, open sh into next open sh; rep from *, ss into 3rd ch.

9th rnd: ss across tr and into sp, * open sh into open sh, 3 ch and 2 tr into same open sh, 6 ch, open sh into next open sh, 3 ch and 1 dc into each of next 2 sp, 3 ch, open sh into open sh, 3 ch and 1 dc into each of next 2 sp, open sh into open sh, 6 ch; rep from *, ss into 3rd ch.

10th rnd: ss across tr and into sp, * open sh into open sh, 2 ch, open sh into next sp, 6 ch, open sh into next open sh, 3 ch and 1 dc into each of next 3 sp, 3 ch, open sh into open sh, 3 ch and 1 dc into each of next 3 sp, 3 ch, open sh into next open sh, 6 ch; rep from *, ss into 3rd ch.

11th rnd: ss across tr and into sp, * open sh into open sh, 4 ch, open sh into next open sh, 6 ch, open sh into open sh, 3 ch and 1 dc into each of next 4 sp, 3 ch, open sh into open sh, 3 ch and 1 dc into each of next 4 sp, 3 ch, open sh into next open sh, 6 ks; rep from *, ss into 3rd ch.

12th and 13th rnds: As 11th rnd, but work 7 ch between open sh.

14th rnd: ss across and into next sp, * open sh into open sh, 5 ch, open sh into next open sh, 7 ch, (open sh into next open sh, 3 ch 1 dc into each of next 2 sp, 3 ch, 1 unf tr into each of next 3 sps, yoh and draw through all lps on hook, 3 ch 1 dc into each of next 2 sp, 3 ch, open sh into open sh) twice, 7 ch; rep from *, ss into 3rd ch.

15th rnd: ss across tr and into sp, * 1 open sh 3 ch and 2 tr into open sh, 3 ch 1 dc into 5 ch sp, 3 ch, 1 open sh 3 ch and 2 tr into next open sh, 7 ch, open sh into open sh, (3 ch, 1 dc into each of next 2 sp, 3 ch, 1 unf tr into each of next 2 sp, yoh and draw through all lps on hook, 3 ch, 1 dc into each of next 2 sp, 3 ch, open sh into open sh) twice; rep from *, ss into 3rd ch.

16th rnd: ss across tr and into sp, * open sh into open sh, 2 ch, open sh into next sp, 3 ch, open sh into next open sh, 2 ch, open sh into next sp, 7 ch, (1 open sh 3 ch and 2 tr into next open sh, 4 ch, 1 unf tr into each of next 2 sp, 3 ch, 1 unf tr into each of next 2 sp, 3 ch, 1 unf tr into each of next 2 sp, 4 ch) twice, 7 ch; rep from *, ss into 3rd ch.

17th rnd: ss across tr and into sp, 7 ch into ss, ss into 4th ch from hook (= 1st tr and p), 1 tr 1 tr and p, 1 tr 1 tr and p into same sp, 2 ch, work in same manner into next 3 open sh, 3 ch, 1 dc into 7 ch sp, 3 ch, (work in same manner into next 2 open sh as in previous 4 open sh, 1 dc into lock st of 2 tr, 1 p on dc, 2 ch, 1 dc 1 p into next lock st, 2 ch, 1 dc 1 p into next lock st, 4 ch) twice. Complete rnd as explained, ss into 3rd ch. Fasten off.

Butterfly
(see photograph 11, p. 22)

MATERIALS: Approximately 30 g Madeira no. 5; crochet hook 1,75 mm

SIZE: 24 cm in diameter

Commence with 10 ch, join with ss to form a ring.

1st rnd: 3 ch into ss, 20 tr into ring, ss into 3rd ch.

2nd rnd: 3 ch into ss, 1 tr each into next 2 tr but keep last lp of each st on hook, yoh and draw through all lps on hook (= 3 tr cl), * 5 ch, 3 tr cl over next 3 tr; rep from *, ss in top of 1st cl.

3rd rnd: ss into sp, 4 dc 6 ch and 4 dc into each sp, ss into 1st dc.

4th rnd: ss across 3 dc and 3 ch to centre of lp, 1 dc into same sp, * 10 ch, 1 dc into next lp; rep from *, ss into 1st dc.

5th rnd: ss into sp, 6 dc 6 ch and 6 dc into each sp around, ss into 1st dc.

6th rnd: ss across 5 dc and into lp, 3 ch into ss (= 1st tr), 4 tr 2 ch and 5 tr into same lp, * 7 ch, 5 tr 2 ch and 5 tr into next lp; rep from *, ss into 3rd ch.

7th rnd: 3 ch into ss, * 1 tr each into next 4 tr, 2 tr 2 ch and 2 tr into sp, 1 tr each into next 5 tr, 2 ch, 1 tr into sp, 2 ch, 1 tr into next tr; rep from *, ss into 3rd ch.

8th rnd: 3 ch into ss, * 1 tr each into next 6 tr, 2 tr 2 ch and 2 tr into sp, 1 tr

Photograph 11: Butterfly

into each of next 7 tr, 2 ch, 1 tr into tr, 2 ch, 1 tr into next tr; rep from *, ss into 3rd ch.

9th rnd: As 8th rnd, but inc as before.

10th rnd: 3 ch into ss, * 1 tr each into next 10 tr, 2 tr 2 ch and 2 tr into sp, 1 tr each into next 11 tr, 1 ch, 1 tr into tr, 1 ch, 1 tr into next tr; rep from *, ss into 3rd ch.

11th rnd: 3 ch into ss, * 1 tr into each of next 11 tr, 2 ch, miss next tr, 1 tr into sp, 2 ch, miss next tr, 1 tr into next tr; rep from *, ss into 3rd ch.

12th rnd: 4 ch into ss (= 1 tr and 1 ch), * miss 1 tr, 1 tr each into next 9 tr, 2 ch, miss next tr, 1 tr into sp, 2 ch, 1 tr into next sp, 2 ch, miss next tr, 1 tr

each into next 9 tr, 1 ch, miss next tr, (1 tr into next tr, 1 ch) 3 times; rep from *, ss into 3rd of 4 ch.

13th rnd: ss across 1 ch and into tr, 3 ch into ss, * 1 tr into each of next 7 tr, 2 ch, miss next tr, 1 tr into sp, 2 ch, 1 tr 2 ch and 1 tr into next sp, 2 ch, 1 tr into sp, 2 ch, miss next tr, 1 tr each into next 8 tr, 5 ch, miss four 1 ch sps, 1 tr into next tr; rep from *, ss into 3rd ch.

14th rnd: 3 ch into ss, * 1 tr each into next 6 tr, 2 ch, miss next tr, (1 tr into next sp 2 ch) twice, 1 tr 2 ch and 1 tr into next sp (2 ch, 1 tr into next sp) twice, 2 ch, miss next tr, 1 tr each into next 7 tr, 2 ch 1 dc and 2 ch into 5 ch

sp, 1 tr into next tr; rep from *, ss into 3rd ch.

15th rnd: 8 ch into ss (= 1 tr and 5 ch), * miss next 5 tr, 1 tr into next tr, (2 ch, 1 tr into sp) 3 times, 2 ch, 1 tr 2 ch and 1 tr into next sp, (2 ch, 1 tr into next sp) 3 times, 2 ch, 1 tr into next tr, 5 ch, miss 5 tr, 1 tr into next tr, 5 ch, 1 tr into next tr; rep from *, ss into 3rd of 8 ch.

16th rnd: 6 ch into ss, 1 dc and 3 ch into 5 ch sp, 1 tr into next tr, 3 ch, 1 dc into next tr, 3 ch, 1 tr into tr, 3 ch, 1 dc into next tr, 3 ch, 1 tr into tr, 3 ch, 1 dc into sp, 3 ch, 1 tr into tr and complete rnd in this manner, ss into 3rd of 6 ch. Fasten off.

Photograph 12: Wheel of fire

Wheel of fire

(see photograph 12, p. 23)

MATERIALS: Approximately 50 g Madeira no. 5; crochet hook 1,75 mm

SIZE: 29 cm in diameter

Commence with 6 ch, join with ss to form a ring.

1st rnd: 1 dc into ss, (5 ch 1 dc into ring) 8 times, ss into 1st dc.

2nd rnd: ss into 5 ch sp, 3 dc into same sp, * 3 ch, 3 dc into next sp; rep from *, ss into 1st dc.

3rd rnd: ss into next dc, 3 ch into ss (= 1st tr), 1 tr into next dc, * 2 tr into sp, 3 ch, miss next dc, 1 tr each into next 2 dc; rep from *, ss into 3rd ch.

4th rnd: ss into next tr, 3 ch into ss, 1 tr each into next 2 tr, * 2 tr into sp, 3 ch, miss next tr, 1 tr each into next 3 tr; rep from *, ss into 3rd ch.

5th rnd: As 4th rnd.

6th rnd: As 5th rnd, but work 4 ch instead of 3.

7th rnd: 3 ch into ss, 1 tr into each of next 5 tr, * 5 ch, miss next tr, 2 tr into sp, 1 tr each into next 6 tr; rep from *, ending with 2 tr into sp, ss into 3rd ch.

8th rnd: As 7th rnd, but work 6 ch instead of 5, ending with 2 tr into sp, 1 tr each into next 2 tr, ss into 3rd ch.

9th to 11th rnd: As 7th rnd, but inc 1 ch in each rnd and work tr gps as explained.

12th rnd: 3 ch into ss, 1 tr into next tr, * 2 tr into sp, 9 ch, miss next tr, 1 tr each into next 11 tr; rep from *, ending with 9 tr, ss into 3rd ch.

13th rnd: 3 ch into ss, 1 tr each into next 3 tr, * 2 tr into sp, 10 ch, miss next tr, 1 tr each into next 12 tr; rep from *, ending with 8 tr, ss into 3rd ch.

14th rnd: 3 ch into ss, 1 tr each into next 4 tr, * 6 ch, miss next tr, 1 dc into 10 ch lp, 6 ch, miss next tr, 1 tr each into next 12 tr; rep from *, ending with 7 tr, ss into 3rd ch.

15th rnd: 3 ch into ss, 1 tr into each of next 3 tr, * 4 ch, miss next tr, 1 dc into lp, 4 ch, 1 dc 4 ch and 1 dc into dc, 4 ch, 1 dc into next lp, 4 ch, miss next tr, 1 tr each into next 10 tr; rep from *, ending with 6 tr, ss into 3rd ch.

16th rnd: 3 ch into ss, 1 tr each into next 2 tr, * 4 ch, miss next tr, 1 dc into

sp, 4 ch, 1 dc into next sp, 2 ch, (1 tr 2 ch) 5 times into next sp, 1 dc into next sp, 4 ch, 1 dc into next sp, 4 ch, miss next tr, 1 tr into each of next 8 tr; rep from *, ending with 5 tr, ss into 3rd ch.

17th rnd: 3 ch into ss, 1 tr into next tr, * (4 ch 1 dc) twice, 2 ch, (1 tr into next tr, 1 tr into sp) 5 times, 2 ch, (1 dc 4 ch) twice, miss next tr, 1 tr each into next 6 tr; rep from *, ending with 4 tr, ss into 3rd ch.

18th rnd: 7 ch into ss, complete as 17th rnd ending with ss into 3rd of 7 ch.

19th rnd: ss across first 2 ch, 1 dc into same sp, * 4 ch, 1 dc into next sp, 2 ch, 1 tr 1 ch into each of next 17 tr, 2 ch, 1 dc into next sp, 4 ch, 1 dc into next sp, 4 ch, miss next tr, 1 tr into each of next 2 tr, 4 ch, miss next tr, 1 dc into next sp; rep from *, ending with 1 ch and 1 tr into 1st dc.

20th rnd: 1 dc into lp made, 3 ch 1 dc into each sp with 1 dc between 2 tr in top of tr gps, ss into 1st dc. Fasten off.

Fan motif with picot edging

(see photograph 13, p. 25)

MATERIALS: Approximately 50 g Madeira no. 5; crochet hook 1,75 mm

SIZE: 28 cm in diameter

Commence with 10 ch, join with ss to form a ring.

1st rnd: 3 ch (= 1st tr), 29 tr into ring, ss into 3rd ch (= 30 tr).

2nd rnd: 1 dc and 2 ch into ss, * miss next tr, 1 dc into next tr, 2 ch, rep from *, ending with 2 ch, ss into 1st dc.

3rd rnd: ss into first 2 ch sp, 3 ch and 2 unf tr into same sp but keep last lp of each st on hook, yoh and draw through all lps on hook (= a 3 tr cl), 4 ch, ss into 1st ch (= p on cl), * 3 ch, 3 tr cl and 1 p into next 2 ch sp; rep

from *, ending with 1 ch and 1 htr in top of 1st cl (= 15 cls).

4th rnd: 1 dc into sp made, * 6 ch, 1 dc into next sp; rep from *, ending with 3 ch and 1 tr into 1st dc.

5th rnd: 1 dc into lp just made, * 7 ch, 1 dc into next sp; rep from *, ending with 3 ch and 1 dtr into 1st dc.

6th rnd: As 5th rnd but end with 7 ch, ss into 1st dc.

7th rnd: ss into 1st sp, 3 ch and 8 tr into sp; rep all round with 9 tr into each sp.

8th rnd: ss across and into 5th tr, 3 ch 1 tr 1 ch and 2 tr into same sp as ss, 3 ch, * 1 unf tr into same sp as previous tr, miss next 4 tr, 1 unf tr into sp between 9 tr gps, miss next 4 tr, 1 unf tr into next tr, yoh and draw through all

lps on hook, 3 ch 2 tr 1 ch and 2 tr into same sp as last unf tr, 3 ch; rep from *, ending with 1 unf tr into same sp as first 4 tr gp, 3 ch, ss into 3rd ch.

9th rnd: 3 ch into ss, * 2 tr into next tr, 1 ch, 2 tr into next tr, 1 tr into next tr, 3 ch, 1 unf tr into same tr as last tr, 1 unf tr into lock st of 3 unf tr of previous rnd, 1 unf tr into next tr, 3 ch, 1 tr into next tr; rep from *, ending as 8th rnd.

10th rnd: As 9th rnd, but work 4 tr gps and 2 ch between tr.

11th rnd: Work exactly as 10th rnd.

12th rnd: 4 tr cl over first 4 tr (3 ch = 1 tr), * 3 ch, 4 tr cl over next 4 tr, 5 ch, 1 unf tr into 3 ch sp, 1 unf tr into next 3 ch sp, yoh and draw through all lps on hook, 5 ch, 4 tr cl over 4 tr; rep

Photograph 13: Fanned edge (front) and fan motif with picot edging (back)

from *, ending with 5 ch, ss in top of 1st cl.

13th rnd: ss across and into 3 ch sp between cl, 3 ch and 7 tr into sp, * 10 ch, miss two 5 ch sp, 8 tr into next 3 ch sp; rep from *, ss into 3rd ch.

14th rnd: 3 ch and 1 tr into same sp as ss, * 1 tr each into next 6 tr, 2 tr into next tr (= 10 tr), 4 ch, insert hook into lock st of 2 tr and around 10 ch lp and work 1 dc, 4 ch, ss into 1st ch (= p on

dc), 4 ch, 2 tr, into next tr; rep from *, ss into 3rd ch.

15th rnd: 3 ch and 1 tr into same sp as ss, * 1 tr each into next 8 tr, 2 tr into next tr (= 12 tr), 7 ch, 2 tr into next tr; rep from *, ss into 3rd ch.

16th rnd: 3 ch into ss, 1 tr into next tr, * (1 ch, 1 tr each into next 2 tr) 5 times (= six 2 tr gps over 12 tr), 7 ch, 1 tr each into next 2 tr; rep from *, ss into 3rd ch.

17th rnd: 3 ch into ss, 1 tr into next tr, *(2 ch, 1 tr into each of next 2 tr) 5 times, 3 ch, 1 dc around both lps of previous 2 rnds, 4 ch, ss into 1st ch (= p on dc), 3 ch, 1 tr each into next 2 tr; rep from *, ss into 3rd ch.

18th rnd: 2 tr cl over first 2 tr, 4 ch, ss into 1st ch (= p on cl), * (3 ch, 2 tr cl over next 2 tr, 1 p on cl) 5 times, 1 ch, 2 tr cl over next 2 tr; rep from *, ss into 1st cl. Fasten off.

Fanned edge
(see photograph 13, p. 25)

MATERIALS: Approximately 50 g Madeira no. 5; crochet hook 1,75 mm

SIZE: 33 cm in diameter

Commence with 12 ch, join with ss to form a ring.

1st rnd: 3 ch (= 1st tr) into ss, 2 tr into ring but keep last lp of each on hook, yoh and draw through all lps on hook (= 3 tr cl), (6 ch 3 tr cl into ring) 7 times, ss into 1st cl, thus 8 cl into ring.

2nd rnd: ss across 2 ch and into sp, 6 ch and 1 tr into same sp, * 8 ch, 1 tr 3 ch and 1 tr into next sp; rep from *, ss into 3rd of 6 ch.

3rd rnd: ss into sp, 6 ch and 1 tr into same sp, * 3 ch, 1 tr 5 ch and 1 tr into next sp, 3 ch, 1 tr 3 ch and 1 tr into next sp; rep from *, ss into 3rd of 6 ch.

4th rnd: ss into sp, 6 ch and 1 tr into same sp, * 3 ch, miss 3 ch sp, 6 tr into 5 ch sp, 3 ch, miss 3 ch sp, 1 tr 3 ch and 1 tr into next 3 ch sp; rep from *, ss into 3rd of 6 ch.

5th rnd: ss into sp, 6 ch and 1 tr into same sp, * 2 ch, 1 tr into next tr, 2 tr into next tr, 1 tr into next tr, 2 ch, 4 tr over next 3 tr, 2 ch, 1 tr 3 ch and 1 tr into next 3 ch sp; rep from *, ss into 3rd of 6 ch.

6th rnd: ss into sp, 6 ch and 1 tr into same sp, * 2 ch, 4 tr cl over 4 tr, 3 ch, 5 tr into next sp, 3 ch, 4 tr cl over 4 tr, 2 ch, 1 tr 3 ch and 1 tr into next 3 ch sp; rep from *, ss into 3rd of 6 ch.

7th rnd: ss into sp, 6 ch and 1 tr into same sp, * 2 ch, 3 tr into next 3 ch sp, 2 ch 1 tr into each of next 5 tr, 2 ch, 3

tr into sp, 2 ch, 1 tr 3 ch and 1 tr into next 3 ch sp; rep from *, ss into 3rd of 6 ch.

8th rnd: ss into sp, 6 ch and 1 tr into same sp, * 3 ch, 3 tr cl over 3 tr, 3 ch, 1 tr each into next 5 tr, 3 ch, 3 tr cl over 3 tr, 3 ch, 1 tr 3 ch and 1 tr into next 3 ch sp; rep from *, ss into 3rd of 6 ch.

9th rnd: ss into sp, 6 ch and 1 tr into same sp, * 5 ch, 1 dc in top of cl, 6 ch, 5 tr cl over 5 tr, 6 ch, 1 dc in top of next cl, 5 ch, 1 tr 3 ch and 1 tr into next 3 ch sp; rep from *, ss into 3rd of 6 ch.

10th rnd: ss into sp, 3 ch (= 1st tr) into ss, 1 tr 2 ch 2 tr 2 ch and 2 tr into same sp, * 5 ch, miss next sp, 1 dc into next sp, 5 ch, 1 dc in top of 5 tr cl, 5 ch, 1 dc into next sp, 5 ch, miss next sp, 2 tr 2 ch 2 tr 2 ch and 2 tr into 3 ch sp; rep from *, ss into 3rd ch.

11th rnd: ss across tr and into sp, 3 ch 1 tr 2 ch and 2 tr into same sp, 2 ch, 2 tr 2 ch and 2 tr into next sp (= open sh), * 6 ch, miss next sp, 1 dc into next sp, 6 ch, 1 dc into next sp, 6 ch, miss next sp, 1 open sh into next sp, 2 ch, 1 open sh into next sp; rep from *, ss into 3rd ch.

12th rnd: ss into open sh, open sh into open sh, (3 ch = 1st tr), * 2 ch, open sh into 2 ch sp, 2 ch, open sh into open sh, 8 ch, miss next sp, 1 dc into next sp, 8 ch, open sh into open sh; rep from *, ss into 3rd ch.

13th rnd: ss into open sh, * (open sh into open sh, 3 ch) 3 times, 6 ch, 1 dc into sp, 1 dc into next dc, 1 dc into

sp, 6 ch; rep from *, ss into 3rd ch.

14th rnd: ss into open sh, * (open sh into open sh, 4 ch) 3 times, 6 ch, 1 dc into sp, 3 dc over 3 dc, 1 dc into next sp, 6 ch; rep from *, ss into 3rd ch.

15th rnd: ss into open sh, * open sh into open sh, 5 ch, open sh 2 ch and 2 tr into next open sh, 5 ch, open sh into next open sh, 8 ch, 1 dc into sp, 5 dc over 5 dc, 1 dc into next sp, 8 ch; rep from *, ss into 3rd ch.

16th rnd: ss into open sh, * open sh into open sh, 6 ch, open sh into next open sh, 3 ch, open sh into next 2 ch sp, 6 ch, open sh into next open sh, 9 ch, miss 1st dc, 5 dc over next 5 dc, 9 ch, miss next dc; rep from *, ss into 3rd ch.

17th rnd: ss into open sh, * open sh into open sh, 6 ch, open sh into next open sh, 4 ch, open sh into next open sh, 6 ch, open sh into open sh, 10 ch, miss 1st dc, 3 dc over 3 dc, 10 ch, miss next dc; rep from *, ss into 3rd ch.

18th rnd: ss into open sh, * open sh into open sh, 7 ch, open sh into next open sh, 5 ch, open sh into next open sh, 7 ch, open sh into open sh, 10 ch, miss 1st dc, 1 dc into next dc, 10 ch, miss next dc; rep from *, ss into 3rd ch.

19th rnd: ss into open sh, * (3 tr 4 ch and 3 tr into open sh, 4 ch, 1 dc into 7 ch sp, 4 ch and ss into 1st ch = p on dc, 4 ch) 4 times, 1 ch, 3 tr, 4 ch and 3 tr into next open sh, 4 ch, 1 dc and p into 7 ch sp, 4 ch; rep from *, ss into 3rd ch. Fasten off.

Flowered doily

(see photograph on front cover)

Pingouin crochet cotton no. 8 (50 g)
1 ball of chosen colour, 30 g makes one cloth; crochet hook 1,25 mm

MEASUREMENT: 30 cm in diameter

Commence with 10 ch, join with ss to form a ring.
1st rnd: 3 ch = 1st tr, into ss, 31 tr into ring (32 tr) ss into 3rd ch.
2nd rnd: 3 ch into ss, 1 tr into next tr, * 1 ch, 1 tr into each of next 4 tr *, rep from * to *, ending with 2 tr, ss into 3rd ch.
3rd rnd: 3 ch and 1 tr into ss, 2 tr into next tr, * 1 ch, 2 tr into next tr, 2 tr into next tr *, rep from * to *, ending with (2 tr into next tr) twice, 1 ch, ss into 3rd ch.
4th rnd: 3 ch into ss, * 1 tr into each of next 3 tr, 2 ch, 1 tr into 1 ch sp, 2 ch, 1 tr into each of next 4 tr, 1 ch, 1 tr into next tr *, rep from * to *, ending with 1 ch, ss into 3rd ch.
5th rnd: 3 ch into ss, 1 tr into each of next 3 tr, * (2 ch, 1 tr into sp) twice, 2 ch, 1 tr into each of next 4 tr, 1 ch, 1 tr into each of next 4 tr *, rep from * to *, ss into 3rd ch.
6th to 11th rnd: As 5th rnd, but inc between tr gps as described above, in 11th rnd there should be 9 sps between tr gps.

12th rnd: ss into tr, 3 ch = 1st tr, 1 tr into each of next 2 tr, * 1 tr into sp, (2 ch, 1 tr into next sp) 7 times, 2 ch, 1 tr into next sp, 1 tr into each of next 3 tr, 4 ch, miss next tr 1 ch and 1 tr, 1 tr into each of next 3 tr *, rep from * to *, ending with 4 ch, ss into 3rd ch.
13th rnd: ss into tr, 3 ch, 1 tr into each of next 2 tr, * 1 tr into sp, (2 ch, 1 tr into next sp) 6 times, 2 ch, 1 tr into next sp, 1 tr into each of next 3 tr, 2 ch, miss next tr, 2 tr 2 ch and 2 tr into 4 ch sp, 2 ch, miss next tr, 1 tr into each of next 3 tr *, rep from * to *, ending with 2 ch, ss into 3rd ch.
14th rnd: ss into tr, 3 ch, 1 tr into each of next 2 tr, * 1 tr into sp, (2 ch, 1 tr into next sp) 5 times, 2 ch, 1 tr into next sp, 1 tr into each of next 3 tr, 2 ch, miss next tr, 2 tr into each of next 2 tr (= 4 tr), 4 ch, 2 tr into each of next 2 tr (= 4 tr), 2 ch, miss next tr, 1 tr into each of next 3 tr *, rep from * to *, ending with 2 ch, ss into 3rd ch.
15th rnd: ss into tr, 1 tr into each of next 2 tr, * 1 tr into sp, (2 ch, 1 tr into next sp) 4 times, 2 ch, 1 tr into next sp, 1 tr into each of next 3 tr, 2 ch, miss next tr, 1 tr into each of next 4 tr, 2 ch, 2 tr 2 ch and 2 tr into 4 ch sp, 2 ch, 1 tr into each of next 4 tr, 2 ch, miss next tr, 1 tr into each of next 3 tr *, rep from * to *, ending with 2 ch, ss

into 3rd ch.
16th rnd: As 14th rnd, but dec as in previous rnds.
17th rnd: As 15th rnd, but dec as in previous rnds.
18th rnd: As 16th rnd, continue to dec.
19th rnd: ss into tr, 1 tr into each of next 2 tr, * 1 tr into sp, 2 ch, 1 tr into next sp, 1 tr into each of next 3 tr, (2 ch, miss next tr, 1 tr into each of next 4 tr) 3 times, 2 ch, 2 tr 2 ch and 2 tr into 4 ch sp, (2 ch, 1 tr into each of next 4 tr) 3 times, 2 ch, miss next tr, 1 tr into each of next 3 tr *, rep from * to *, ending with 2 ch, ss into 3rd ch.
20th rnd: ss into tr, 1 tr into each of next 2 tr, 1 tr into sp (keep last st of each tr on hook, yoh and draw through all lps on hook) = 4 tr cl, 4 ch, ss into 1st ch, 1 p on cl, 1 ch, 1 tr into sp, 1 tr into each of next 3 tr, keep last lps on hook, yoh and draw through all lps on hook, 1 p on cl, 5 ch, 1 dc into sp, 5 ch, (4 tr cl over next 4 tr, 1 p, 5 ch, 1 dc into next sp, 5 ch) 3 times, 4 tr cl into 4 ch sp, 1 p on tr, 5 ch, 1 ch into next sp, 5 ch, (4 tr cl over next 4 tr, 1 p, 5 ch, 1 ch into sp, 5 ch) 3 times. Complete rnd. Fasten off.

Jolly cloth

(see photograph 14, p. 28)

Pingouin crochet cotton no. 8 (50 g), One ball of selected colour, 30 g makes one cloth; crochet hook 1,25 mm

MEASUREMENT: 28 cm in diameter

Commence with 8 ch, join with ss to form a ring.
1st rnd: 3 ch into ss = 1st tr, 3 tr into ring, (2 ch, 4 tr into ring) 7 times.
2nd rnd: [4 tr over 4 tr (keep last lp on hook, yoh, and draw through all lps on hook) 8 ch] 7 times, ss into top of 1st cl.

3rd rnd: 3 ch and 1 tr into top of cl, * 5 ch 1 dc and 5 ch into 8 ch sp, 2 tr into top of next cl *, rep from * to *, ss into 3rd ch.
4th rnd: 3 ch and 1 tr into ss, * 2 tr into next tr, 4 ch, 1 tr into each of next 2 sps, 4 ch, 2 tr into next tr *, rep from * to *, ss into 3rd ch.
5th rnd: 4 tr cl over 4 tr, * 4 ch, 1 dc into sp, 8 ch, 1 dc into next sp, 4 ch, 4 tr cl over next 4 tr *, rep from * to *, ss into top of 1st cl.
6th rnd: 3 ch and 1 tr into ss, * 3 ch, miss next sp, 4 tr 3 ch and 4 tr into next sp, 3 ch, miss next sp, 2 tr into

top of cl *, rep from * to *, ss into 3rd ch.
7th rnd: 3 ch and 1 tr into ss, * 2 tr into next tr, 4 ch, 4 tr cl over next 4 tr, 4 ch, 4 tr into sp, 4 ch, 4 tr cl over next 4 tr, 4 ch, 2 tr into next tr *, rep from * to *, ss into 3rd ch.
8th rnd: * 4 tr cl over 4 tr, 6 ch, 1 dc into sp, 8 ch, 4 tr cl over next 4 tr, 8 ch, miss next sp, 1 dc into next sp, 6 ch *, rep from * to *, ss into top of 1st cl.
9th rnd: 3 ch and 1 tr into ss, 6 ch, * 1 tr into each of next 2 sps, 8 ch 2 tr into top of next cl, 8 ch, 1 tr into each of

next 2 sps, 6 ch, 2 tr into top of next cl, 6 ch *, rep from * to *, ss into 3rd ch.

10th rnd: 3 ch and 1 tr into ss, * 2 tr into next tr, 3 ch, 1 dc into sp, 3 ch, 1 dc into next sp, 3 ch, 2 tr into next tr *, rep from * to *, ss into 3rd ch.

11th rnd: * 4 tr cl over 4 tr, 4 ch, miss sp, 4 tr 2 ch and 4 cl into next sp, 4 ch, miss next sp *, rep from * to *, ss into top of 1st cl.

12th rnd: 3 ch and 1 tr into ss, * 3 ch, 4 tr cl over 4 tr, 3 ch, 4 tr into sp, 3 ch, 4 tr cl over next 4 tr, 3 ch, 2 tr into top of next cl *, rep from * to *, ss into 3rd ch.

13th rnd: 3 ch and 1 tr into ss, 2 tr into next tr, * 8 ch, 4 tr cl over 4 tr, 8 ch, 2 tr into each of next tr (= 4 tr) *, rep from * to *, ss into 3rd ch.

14th rnd: * 4 tr cl over 4 tr, 4 ch 1 dc 4 ch into 8 ch sp, 2 tr into top of cl, 4 ch 1 dc and 4 ch into next 8 ch sp *, rep from * to *, ss into top of 1st cl.

15th rnd: 3 ch and 1 tr into ss, * 4 ch, 1 tr into each of next 2 sps, 4 ch, 2 tr into each of next 2 tr (= 4 tr), 4 ch, 1 tr into each of next 2 sps, 4 ch, 2 tr into top of next cl *, rep from * to *, ss into 3rd ch.

16th rnd: 3 ch and 1 tr into ss, 2 tr into next tr, * 3 ch, 1 dc into sp, 4 ch, 1 dc into next sp, 3 ch, 4 tr cl over 4 tr, 3 ch, 1 dc into sp, 4 ch, 1 dc into next sp, 3 ch, 2 tr into each of next 2 tr (= 4 tr) *, rep from * to *, ss into 3rd ch.

17th rnd: * 4 tr cl over 4 tr, 2 ch, miss next sp, 4 tr 3 ch and 4 tr into next sp, 2 ch, 2 tr into top of cl, 2 ch, miss next sp, 4 tr 3 ch and 4 tr into next sp, 2 ch *, rep from * to *, ss into top of 1st cl.

18th rnd: 3 ch and 1 tr into top of cl, * 3 ch, 4 tr cl over 4 tr, 3 ch 4 tr and 3 ch into sp, 4 tr cl over next 4 tr, 3 ch, 2 tr into each of next 2 tr (= 4 tr), 3 ch, 4 tr cl, 3 ch 4 tr and 3 ch into sp, 4 tr cl, 3 ch, 2 tr into top of next cl *, rep from * to *, ss into 3rd ch.

19th rnd: 1 dc into ss, * (8 ch, 4 tr cl over next 4 tr) 3 times, 8 ch, 1 dc between next 2 tr *, rep from * to *, ss into 1st dc.

20th rnd: 4 dc 3 ch and 4 dc into each 8 ch sp, ss into 1st dc. Fasten off.

Photograph 14: Jolly cloth

Like a cobweb

(see photograph 15, p. 30)

Fiesta crochet cotton no. 5 (50 g), 1 ball of selected colour, 20 g makes one cloth; crochet hook 1,75 mm.

MEASUREMENT: 25 cm in diameter

Commence with 8 ch, join with ss to form a ring.

1st rnd: 21 dc into ss, ss into 1st dc.
2nd rnd: 3 ch into ss = 1st tr, 1 tr into each of next 2 dc, * 3 ch, 1 tr into each of next 3 dc *, rep from * to *, ss into 3rd ch.
3rd rnd: 3 ch, 1 tr into each of next 2 tr, * 5 ch, 1 tr into each of next 3 tr *, rep from * to *, ss into 3rd ch.
4th rnd: 3 ch into ss, 1 tr into each of next 2 tr, * 3 ch, 1 tr 3 ch and 1 tr into sp, 3 ch, 1 tr into each of next 3 tr *, rep from * to *, ss into 3rd ch.
5th rnd: 3 ch into ss, 1 tr into each of next 2 tr, * 4 ch, miss next sp, 1 tr 3 ch and 1 tr into next sp, 4 ch, 1 tr into each of next 3 tr *, rep from * to *, ss into 3rd ch.
6th rnd: 3 ch into ss, 1 tr into each of next 2 tr, * 2 ch, (1 tr 1 ch) 7 times into 3 ch sp, 2 ch, 1 tr into each of next 3 tr *, rep from * to *, ss into 3rd ch.

7th rnd: 3 ch into ss, 1 tr into each of next 2 tr, * 3 ch, 1 dc 3 ch and 1 dc into next tr, 5 ch, miss next 2 tr, 1 tr 3 ch and 1 tr into next tr, 5 ch, miss next 2 tr, 1 dc 3 ch and 1 dc into next tr, 3 ch, 1 tr into each of next 3 tr *, rep from * to *, ss into 3rd ch.
8th rnd: 3 ch into ss, 1 tr into each of next 2 tr, * 6 ch, 1 dc into 5 ch sp, 5 ch, 1 tr 3 ch and 1 tr into next sp, 5 ch 1 dc into next sp, 6 ch, 1 tr into each of next 3 tr *, rep from * to *, ss into 3rd ch.
9th rnd: 3 ch into ss, 1 tr into each of next 2 tr, * 6 ch, miss 2 sps, (1 tr 1 ch) 9 times into next sp, 6 ch, 1 tr into each of next 4 tr *, rep from * to *, ss into 3rd ch.
10th rnd: 3 ch into ss, 1 tr into each of next 2 tr, * 6 ch, 1 dc 3 ch and 1 dc into next tr, 6 ch, miss 3 tr, 1 tr 5 ch and 1 tr into next tr, 6 ch, miss next 3 tr, 1 dc 3 ch and 1 dc into last tr, 6 ch, 1 tr into each of next 3 tr *, rep from * to *, ss into 3rd ch.
11th rnd: 3 ch into ss, 1 tr into each of next 2 tr, * 10 ch, miss next 2 sps, (1 tr 1 ch) 11 times into 5 ch sp, 10 ch, 1 tr into each of next 3 tr *, rep from * to *, ss into 3rd ch.

12th rnd: 3 ch into ss, 1 tr into each of next 2 tr, * 6 ch 1 dc and 6 ch into 10 ch sp, 1 dc 3 ch and 1 dc into tr, 8 ch, miss 4 tr, 1 tr 5 ch and 1 tr into next 1 tr, 8 ch, miss next 4 tr, 1 dc 3 ch and 1 dc into last tr, 6 ch 1 dc and 6 ch into 10 ch sp, 1 tr into each of next 3 tr *, rep from * to *, ss into 3rd ch.
13th rnd: 3 ch into ss, 1 tr into each of next 2 tr, * 8 ch, miss next sp, 1 dc into next sp, 8 ch, miss next sp, (1 tr 1 ch) 13 times into 5 ch sp, 8 ch, miss next sp, 1 dc into next sp, 8 ch, 1 tr into each of next 3 tr *, rep from * to *, ss into 3rd ch.
14th rnd: 3 ch into ss, 1 tr into each of next 2 tr, (keep last st on hook, yoh and draw through all sts on hook) = 3 tr cl, 4 ch, ss into 1st ch = p on cl, * 3 ch, 6 ch into each of next 2 sps, (1 dc 3 ch and 1 dc into 1 tr, 1 dc into next tr) 7 times, 6 dc into each of next 2 sps, 3 ch, 3 tr cl and p over next 3 tr *, rep from * to *, ss into top of 1st cl. Fasten off.

Cloth with sharp-pointed edge

(see photograph 15, p. 30)

Fiesta crochet cotton no. 5 (50 g), 1 ball of selected colour, 25 g makes one cloth; crochet hook 1,75 mm

MEASUREMENT: 28 cm in diameter

Commence with 6 ch, join with ss to form a ring.

1st rnd: 6 ch into ss = 1 tr + 3 cs, (1 tr 3 ch) 7 times into ring (8 tr).
2nd rnd: ss into sp, 5 tr 1 ch into each sp, ss into 3rd ch.
3rd rnd: Turn work and ss into 1 ch sp, turn back, 3 ch into ss, 3 tr into same sp, * 5 ch, miss 5 tr, 5 tr into next 1 ch sp *, rep from * to *, ss into 3rd ch.
4th rnd: 3 ch into ss, 1 tr into next tr, * 3 ch, 1 tr into each of next 2 tr, 3 ch 1 dc and 3 ch into sp, 1 tr into each of next 2 tr *, rep from * to *, ss into 3rd ch.
5th rnd: ss into sp, 3 ch = 1st tr, 1 tr 3 ch and 2 tr into same sp, * 8 ch, 2 tr 3 ch and 2 tr between next 4 tr *, hereafter referred to as osh (open shell), rep from * to *, ss into 3rd ch.
6th rnd: ss into osh, osh into osh, * 4 ch, 1 dc 3 ch and 1 dc into 8 ch sp, 4 ch, osh into osh *, rep from * to *, ss into 3rd ch.
7th rnd: ss into osh, osh into osh, * 6 ch, 1 dc 3 ch and 1 dc into 3 ch eyelet, 6 ch, osh into osh *, rep from * to *, ss into 3rd ch.
8th rnd: 3 ch into ss, 1 tr into tr, * 3 tr 3 ch and 3 tr into sp, 1 tr into each of next 2 tr, 6 ch, 1 tr into eyelet, 6 ch, 1 tr into each of next 2 tr *, rep from * to *, ss into 3rd ch.
9th rnd: 3 ch into ss, * 1 tr into each of next 4 tr, 3 tr 3 ch and 3 tr into sp, 1 tr into each of next 5 tr, 5 ch, 1 tr into each of next 2 sps, 5 ch, 1 tr into next tr *, rep from * to *, ss into 3rd ch.

29

Photograph 15: Cloth with sharp-pointed edge (front) and like a cobweb (back)

10th rnd: 3 ch into ss, * 1 tr into each of next 7 tr, 3 tr 3 ch and 3 tr into sp, 1 tr into each of next 8 tr, 3 ch, 1 tr into each of next 2 sps, 3 ch, 1 tr into next tr *, rep from * to *, ss into 3rd ch.

11th rnd: 3 ch into ss, * 1 tr into each of next 10 tr, 3 tr 3 ch and 3 tr into sp, 1 tr into each of next 11 tr, 2 ch, 1 tr into each of next 2 sps, 2 ch, 1 tr into next tr *, rep from * to *, ss into 3rd ch.

12th rnd: 3 ch into ss, * 1 tr into each of next 13 tr, 3 tr 3 ch and 3 tr into sp, 1 tr into each of next 14 tr, 1 ch, 1 tr into each of next 2 sps, 1 ch 1 tr into next tr *, rep from * to *, ss into 3rd ch.

13th rnd: 3 ch into ss, * 1 tr into each of next 16 tr, 3 tr, 3 ch and 3 tr into sp, 1 tr into each of next 17 tr, 1 tr into each 1 ch sp, 1 tr into next tr *, rep from * to *, ss into 3rd ch. Fasten off.

Like a net

(see photograph on back cover)

Fiesta crochet cotton no. 5 (50 g), 1 ball of chosen colour, 30 g makes one cloth; crochet hook 1,75 mm

MEASUREMENT: 29 cm in diameter

Commence with 8 ch, join with ss to form a ring.

1st rnd: (1 dc 3 ch) 9 times into ring.

2nd rnd: ss into sp, 1 dc 4 ch into each sp, ending with 2 ch 1 htr into 1st dc.

3rd rnd: 1 dc into sp just formed, 5 ch 1 dc into each sp, ending with 2 ch 1 tr into 1st dc.

4th rnd: 1 dc 6 ch into sp just formed, 1 dc 6 ch into each sp, ss into 1st dc.

5th rnd: ss into sp, 1 dc 4 ch 1 dc 4 ch and 1 dc into same sp, rep into each sp, ss into 1st dc.

6th rnd: ss into sp, 1 dc 6 ch into each sp, ending with 3 ch 1 tr into 1st dc.

7th rnd: 1 dc into sp just formed, 7 ch 1 dc into each sp, ss into 1st dc.

8th rnd: ss over 3 ch of sp, 1 dc 8 ch into each sp, ending with 4 ch 1 dtr into 1st dc.

9th rnd: 1 dc into sp just formed, 9 ch 1 dc into each sp, ss into 1st dc.

10th rnd: 5 ch into ss, * miss 2 ch, 1 tr into next ch *, rep from * to *, ss into 3rd of 5 ch = 61 sps.

11th rnd: ss into sp, 3 ch (= 1st tr) and 2 tr into same sp, 1 ch 3 tr into each sp, ss into 3rd ch.

12th rnd: 3 ch into ss, 1 tr into each of next 2 tr (keep last st of each tr on hook, yoh and draw through all sts on hook) = 3 tr cl, 4 ch, ss into 1st ch to form p on cl, 2 ch, 3 tr cl 1 p and 2 ch into each sp, ss into 1st cl.

13th rnd: ss to 2 ch sp, 1 dc 6 ch into each sp, ending with 3 ch 1 tr into 1st dc.

14th and 15th rnd: Rep 13th rnd.

16 and 17th rnd: 1 dc into sp just formed, 7 ch 1 dc into each sp, ending with 3 ch 1 dtr into 1st dc.

18th rnd: As 17th rnd, but ending with ss into 1st dc.

19th rnd: ss into sp, 7 dc into each sp, ss into 1st dc. Fasten off.

Delos, 40 Heerengracht, Cape Town

Also available in Afrikaans as *Doilies*

Photography by Siegfried Behm
Translated by Hettie Hauman and Elbie Fugler
Book and cover design by Richard Jones
Set in 10 on 11 pt Optima
Printed and bound by National Book Printers, Goodwood, Cape
First edition 1990

ISBN 1-86826-113-1